SAIL

for Racing

fernhurst
BOOKS

SAILS
for Racing

John Heyes

First published 1987, Second edition 1992, Third edition 1998.

Fernhurst Books, Duke's Path, High Street, Arundel, West Sussex, BN18 9AJ.
Tel 01903 882277 Fax 01903 882715.

ISBN 1 898660 50 6

Acknowledgements
The publishers would like to thank all those who sailed in the photo sessions:
The Hyde Sails team (Melges 24); Andy and Ian Budgen (49er); Steve Drakeford and Gordon Kingston (505);
Glyn Charles, Max Walker and Andy Beadsworth (Norman Cunningham's Soling); Rob McMillan (Finn).
Also thanks to Gordon Walker and his crew for allowing photography aboard the Sigma 38 Pavlova, and the
R.O.R.C. Rating Office, Lymington, for the polar diagram on page 82.
The computer-generated diagrams and stress maps on pages 63, 73 and 86 were generated
by Peter Kay of Parker and Kay Sailmakers, using Peter Heppel's 'RELAX' design program.

Photographs
The photographs are by Chris Davies, Rick Tomlinson, Tim Hore and John Woodward, with the exception
of the following: Christel Clear: pages 61, 74, 85
Yachting Photographics: pages 60, 78 (top), Rolex: page 48
Peter Bentley: page 27, J-Boats Inc.: pages 25, 30
Cover photos by Hyde, Peter Bentley, J-Boats Inc.

Design by PanTek, Maidstone and Creative Byte, Poole.

Composition by A & G Phototypesetters, Knaphill, CST Eastbourne and Creative Byte, Poole.

Printed and bound in China through World Print

Contents

1 How sails work

There are many explanations of how a sail works, but most of them seem to assume the reader has a degree in aerodynamics. Since this is a big assumption, we will use a fairly simple concept: that of the sail as an 'air deflector'.

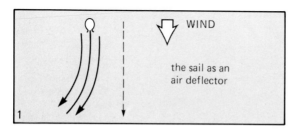

the sail as an air deflector

WIND

In the absence of a sail or other obstacle the wind will usually blow in a straight line (fig. 1). But put a sail in the path of the wind and the airflow is deflected. Some force is obviously at work on the air particles, directing them to the right, and since action and reaction are always equal and opposite the air particles will pull the sail to the left.

Another theory assumes that the air flowing around the lee side of the sail has to travel further than the air on the windward side. This reduces the pressure on the lee side, and the sail is 'sucked' to leeward.

Whichever theory you prefer, the effect is the same: because the sail is made of cloth it will move until the forces on it are acting at right-angles to its surface. Since the sail is curved the forces at each point will act in slightly different directions (fig. 2). For clarity, however, they can be

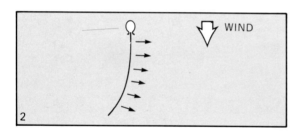

WIND

represented by one large vector arrow (fig. 3). This is the overall (or total) force on the sail: force F.

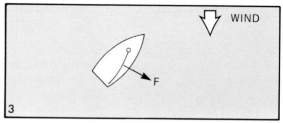

WIND

F can be split into two parts: the part which does useful work thrusting the boat forward (T), and the part which simply pushes the boat sideways (H). H is resisted by the keel or centreboard, with the result that the boat tends to heel over.

The larger the curve (or depth) in the sail, the greater the deflection of the air particles and the greater the power that is developed. F increases and so does T, so the boat will go faster.

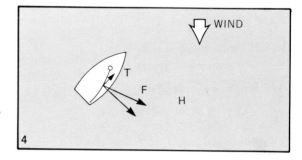

WIND

Unfortunately, H also increases, and there comes a point when the boat will capsize. That is why the mast is bent to flatten the sails and reduce their power in strong winds.

As the boat bears away and the mainsheet is eased (fig. 5) F swings round and points in a more useful direction. In other words, H is reduced and T is increased, so the boat goes forwards faster and with less heel.

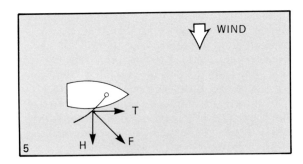

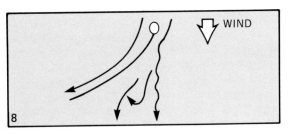

As the boat bears away still more (fig. 6) the wind can no longer flow over the sail and the 'air deflector' effect is lost. It is simply the force of the air hitting the sail that pushes the boat along on a run, and progress is slower than on a beat or a reach.

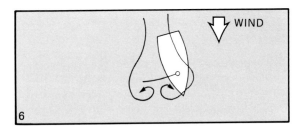

The role of the jib

The jib operates as an air deflector in the same way as the mainsail, but it also performs a vital role in training the airflow across the leeward side of the main. The presence of the jib increases the pressure around the lee side of the mast, which in turn causes a decrease in the apparent wind speed at this point. The slowing of airflow at the luff has two effects:

● The resistance to stall is increased, (because susceptibility to stall is directly related to windspeed).

● The lower apparent windspeed alters the direction of the force on the front of the mainsail. As a result the jib effectively puts the main into a 'header'. This is one reason why the mainsail is sheeted closer to the centreline than the jib, and it makes possible a slightly higher angle of attack and greater thrust.

Break point

If you have ever looked out of an aircraft window as the plane flies through cloud, you may have seen the attached flow over the wing break into turbulent eddies near the trailing edge. The same happens on the leeward side of a sail, beginning at the 'break point' (fig. 7).

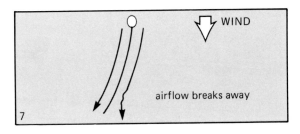

airflow breaks away

Although some separation of flow is inevitable towards the leech of the sail, the objective is to keep this to a minimum and keep the flow attached for as long as possible. That is one reason why oversheeting a sail is so deadly: the deflection expected of the air is too great, the flow breaks away too early, and drive is lost (fig. 8).

Above: A Finn in classic upwind trim. The draft on a una rig is well aft to keep the flow attached as far back as possible, and this results in large sideways forces. To counteract this the boom must be sheeted well down to leeward.

Slot effect

As the jib is sheeted in closer to the main, the velocity of flow through the slot is diminished, until it matches the velocity on the windward side of the main. At this point the slot is acting at maximum efficiency. Thereafter, as the jib is brought in closer to the main, the flow through the slot drops further; the leeside pressure builds up and causes the main to backwind.

Contrary to popular theory, the jib does not serve to speed up flow through the slot, but in fact slows it. Both main and jib work by deflecting the airflow but the slot effect greatly improves the efficiency of the jib, while slightly lowering that of the main. In combination, the thrust of main and jib is greater than that of the two sails working separately. This does however make trimming the sails a harder task, as not only does each sail have to be sheeted to do its own job properly; it also has to be so positioned that it maximises the efficiency of the other.

Una-rigs

The Laser, Finn and O.K. sails work in much the same way as other mainsails, but with one important difference. Normally the break point – the position on the leeward side where the attached flow breaks away from the sail and becomes turbulent flow – coincides with the maximum draft position. Aft of this it becomes

increasingly difficult to keep the flow attached to the sail, and it breaks away and follows the tangent of that part of the curve. On a una-rig boat the break point occurs sooner, owing to the absence of a jib to train the flow around the leeward side. To combat this problem the maximum depth is set a little further aft, in an attempt to keep the flow attached for longer; more importantly the sail is set at a greater angle to the centreline. With the traveller well down to leeward, the overall force on the sail (F) swings forward and the thrust force (T) is increased to an efficient level.

SOME DEFINITIONS

Before discussing sail shapes, it is useful to become familiar with a little terminology.

Aspect ratio

The aspect ratio describes the basic proportions of a sail. The narrower the sail, the higher the aspect ratio. In general, a high-aspect sail provides better upwind performance, as it provides the highest lift and lowest drag. The optimum aspect ratio for beating would have a luff length of three times the foot length, whereas for reaching a much lower-aspect sail is faster. However, the high-aspect rig produces greater heeling forces, as the centre of effort is positioned higher in the sail.

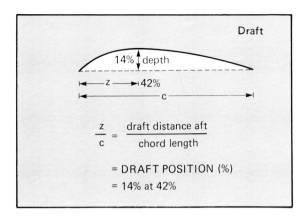

Draft

$$\frac{z}{c} = \frac{\text{draft distance aft}}{\text{chord length}}$$

$$= \text{DRAFT POSITION (\%)}$$

$$= 14\% \text{ at } 42\%$$

Depth

Sail depth is defined as the ratio of the depth of curvature to the chord length. The chord is the line from the leech to the luff. Described in percentage terms, the depth of the sail in the diagram is 14% of the total chord length.

Above: The draft stripes on this Soling enable the draft to be assessed on the water, and from photographs.

Above: Attaching draft stripes. Take a tuck in the sail so it lies flat. Then stick on the stripes parallel to the waterline at the quarter heights.

Draft

The position of greatest depth in the sail, at a particular height, is known as the 'draft position', and is again described in percentage terms of total chord length. The draft in the diagram is located at 42% of the chord length, measured aft from the mast. So a complete description of the sail shape is 14% depth at 42% aft'.

Depth and draft are commonly measured by the sailmaker at the quarter, half and three-quarter heights of the sail. Trim stripes should be marked on the sail at these heights to give the eye a greater appreciation of draft and to serve as a reference when draft is measured from photographs. Trim stripes should be placed on the sail parallel to the waterline, so that the section through the sail is horizontal. Fast sails are generally deeper in the head than in the foot.

Angle of attack

The angle of attack is a measure of the roundness of the luff. A small angle of attack gives a fine entry and good pointing ability. A more rounded entry is less prone to stall, however, and provides more power in waves but results in a lower pointing angle. It is harder to sail with a fine-entried sail, as the difference between luffing and stalling is small; a sail with a more rounded entry is more forgiving as it allows a wider range of headings before the sail luffs or stalls.

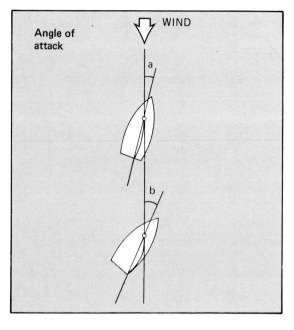

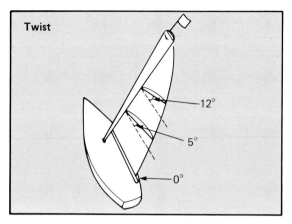

Left: Small angle of attack (a); large angle of attack (b).
Below left and right: To compare the twist in sails take photographs straight down the boom. Draw a line from the head to the clew (1). Then draw a second line at right angles, to the point of maximum twist (2). Express 2 as a percentage of 1, to give the degree of twist.

Above: To record the draft and depth of your sails as shown here, first log the windspeed and wave heights. Then take photographs of the sails from below, using print film. From the prints, measure the depth and draft as a percentage of chord length (there is a proprietary scale available to make this job easier).

Twist

Twist is defined as the variation in chord angle up the sail. It is either described in degrees or, when measuring from photographs, in percentages. The correct amount of twist means that the whole sail will luff at the same time. Much has been written about vertical wind gradients and wind shear demanding more twist on starboard tack than on port, depending on which hemisphere you are in! The greatest windspeed gradient occurs within a frictional layer of a few wave heights, and within the range of a dinghy mast there may be a 5% variation (see Chapter 7).

CLOTH

Sailcloth is described in terms of its weight, finish and stretch characteristics.

Cloth weight

Cloth weight is either measured in US oz/square yard, g/m^2 or occasionally UK oz/square yard, so be careful to check the measure specified in the class rules. The weights of many cloths do not coincide exactly with the weights printed on the labels, as they are product names rather than actual weights. It is worth bearing this point in mind when selecting sail material for a class which restricts the cloth that can be used. '6.O oz Dacron', may in fact weight 5.75 oz, and this may not qualify under the class rules.

Cloth stretch

Cloth stretch plays a vital part in determining the shape of a sail. The sailmaker's main aim is to build a sail which will set in its designed shape in the widest possible range of conditions. If he selects a cloth which is too stretchy, the shape may be perfect in 6 knots of breeze, but a disaster in 15 knots.

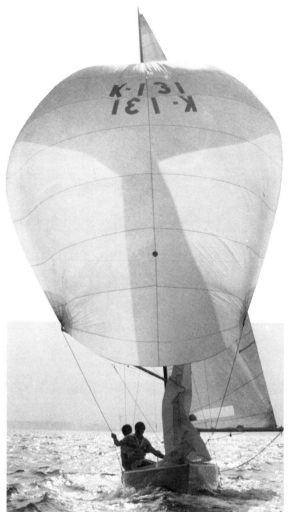

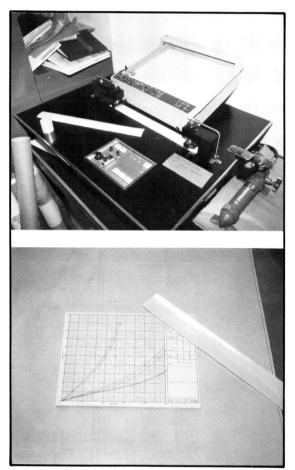

Above: This machine tests the stretch characteristics of cloth in three directions, to ensure the fabric matches the design specifications for the sail. A graph is printed out showing the distortion under load in each stretch direction. A second sample of cloth is then fluttered to simulate use, and the test repeated (giving pairs of lines on the graph).

Cloth is made from threads which run in two directions: the 'warp' threads which run in the long axis of the cloth, and the 'fill' or 'weft' threads which run across the long axis. The amount of stretch in these two directions is mainly governed by the size of the threads and their density of packing, but the warp commonly stretches less. A weaver may set up a warp of 5000 to 10 000 metres, across which the fill threads are woven one at a time and tightly pounded into place. This causes the fill threads to become 'crimped' as they pass alternately under and over the warp. When placed under load, the crimped yarns of the weft straighten out, resulting in much greater stretch in this direction than in the straight warp threads.

The ratio of fill to warp stretch can however be adjusted by altering the relative sizes of the yarns in each direction. For example, the sail designer can choose different threads to match the loads in a cross-cut sail, where the maximum loading is on the leech and is therefore carried by the fill threads. As we have already seen, the continuous warp threads are naturally stronger than the crimped fill fibres. In order for the fill to be the stronger orientation, the fibres must necessarily be larger or more numerous than the warp fibres to withstand the higher loading of the leech.

Bias stretch

The greatest stretch occurs at 45 degrees to the fill and warp, and this is known as the bias direction. Bias stretch is a result of the weave construction. Under load the threads pivot at their intersection points and the rectangular areas between the fibres are pulled into parallelograms. In order to reduce bias stretch, the cloth manufacturer applies a resin dressing to the weave, which impregnates the fibres and glues the threads into position, so reducing the amount of stretch. The stiffness of a cloth is partly determined by how much resin is applied during the finishing process. There are often several finishes available for a particular cloth weight, ranging from soft, via medium firm, to yarn tempered which is the stiffest. The yarn tempered finish is produced by applying considerable resin to the weave and then passing it through heated rollers. Small lines ('crazing') will appear in the sail with use, as the stiff finish cracks where it has been folded, or where the genoa clew hits the mast during tacking.

Below: The large mast bend of the Finn (left) demands a high bias stretch. The 505 mast (right) bends less, so the main can be made of stiffer cloth (yarn tempered or Mylar).

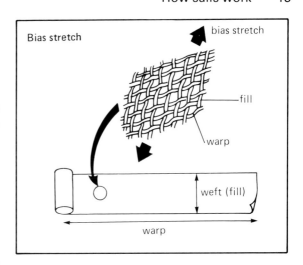

Above: Stretching the cloth in the bias direction pulls the fibres out of square. A resin dressing applied to the weave prevents this happening.

WHICH CLOTH?

The next area to consider is why a sail designer selects a certain fabric for a particular sail. We have already seen that sails of different aspect ratio have different load distributions and hence require different fabrics.

Headsails

As the jib is primarily an up-wind sail, it has to operate in conditions of high apparent wind speed. Furthermore it does not have the benefit of a sail placed in front (as in the case of the mainsail), to slow and train the airflow. For these reasons it is desirable to have a jib which will maintain its shape through the wind range, so the majority of racing classes use jibs or genoas built from a stiff yarn tempered cloth. Another reason for this is to keep to a minimum the extra fullness caused by the forestay sagging to leeward in a breeze.

Mainsails

Mainsails are commonly built from a fairly firm cloth, which has fill threads strong enough to withstand leech loading, but also has sufficient bias stretch at the luff to match the likely range of mast bend. The panel orientation in a cross-cut sail puts the fill threads parallel to the leech and the bias direction parallel to the luff. In the case of a jib, a certain amount of bias stretch is necessary at the luff to make the sail responsive to halyard tension. For a mainsail, bias stretch at the luff is even more important. From the photos you can compare the mast bend of a Finn with that of a 505, which explains why the Finn sailcloth has a high bias stretch. In order to flatten the Finn sail, considerable mast bend is employed. If the bias stretch did not match the range of mast bend, it would be impossible to flatten the sail

and large creases would run from clew to luff. A 505 has a much smaller range of controlled mast bend, and can use a stiffer, less stretchy yarn tempered cloth.

In short, a large part of the sail designers' job is to choose a cloth with the correct stretch characteristics to match the mast bend, aspect ratio and sail shape he wishes to create.

Laminated sailcloths

Mylar* is a trade name for a polyester film which is commonly used for laminated fabrics, in the same way that the name Dacron* is used for woven polyester cloth. Chemically the two are the same. Dacron is extruded as fine filaments which are then spun into thread. Mylar is also extruded, but in long thin sheets which gives the material its uniform directional stretch characteristics. This is the reason Mylar scores over woven fabrics: it eliminates bias stretch. In practice a single film of Mylar is brittle and tears easily. For this reason, sailcloth Mylar consists of a layer of Mylar film bonded onto a woven Dacron substrate. The woven element improves the material's tear strength and flexibility, while the performance of the whole fabric depends upon the strength of the bonding agent. When Mylar first came out the adhesive was the weak link; this often resulted in delamination. Over the years much has been learnt about bonding techniques and Mylar failure is now a thing of the past.

Applications for Mylar

The benefits of reduced weight and stretch and increased durability make Mylar the ideal material for headsails. For mainsails, the weight saving advantage is still relevant, and so too is the reduced stretch factor in the leech. However, with a mainsail made of laminated fabric it is often difficult to remove fullness by bending the mast as the breeze gets up, because there is so little bias stretch. For this reason Mylar mainsails are only effective in those one-design boats which would otherwise use a yarn tempered cloth, such as the 505, which has a small, controlled degree of mast bend. For other classes, laminated sails would only fit a specific mast bend and would have only a very small wind range.

Mylar and Dacron are Dupont registered trademarks

2 Sailmaking

While it is not necessary to know how to build sails to use them, it is useful to have an idea how they are put together when discussing your requirements with the sailmaker. The three shaping elements in a sail are the luff curve, broadseam and cloth stretch.

Luff curve

Before the days of panel shaping, curving the luff was the only method of putting shape into a sail. If a curve is cut on the front of a sail which is then set on a straight mast, the extra cloth forces shape into the sail. Relying on luff curve alone gives the sail a very unsatisfactory draft forward shape, however, and today the shape is created through a combination of luff curve and broadseam.

In the case of the jib, the luff curve becomes luff hollow, cut to match the envisaged luff sag.

Broadseam

The broadseam is simply the curved edge of the cloth panel, which when joined to the straight edge of the adjacent panel forces camber into the sail. Once the sail is seamed up it assumes a three-dimensional shape and will not lie flat on the floor. The amount of broadseam is critical,

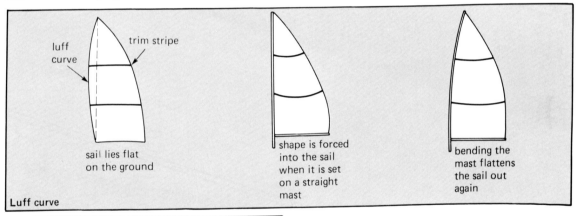

luff curve

trim stripe

sail lies flat on the ground

shape is forced into the sail when it is set on a straight mast

bending the mast flattens the sail out again

Luff curve

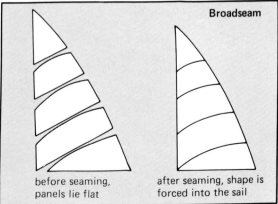

Broadseam

before seaming, panels lie flat

after seaming, shape is forced into the sail

and changes of only a few millimetres can make a dramatic difference to sail shape.

Small vertical darts or 'take-ups' in the foot panel curl the foot round up into a more powerful shape for offwind work.

Cloth stretch

Cloth stretch is an intrinsic part of a sail's design. For example, the most important element of a Finn sail is the cloth. As the wind builds, the bias stretch in the cloth makes the sail fuller in the leech, providing extra power.

MYLAR PATTERNS

Traditionally, one-design sails are built from full size Mylar patterns. Broadseams, battens, luff curve and leech positions are all marked on the Mylar sheet by raised tapes. The cloth is carefully rolled out across the pattern parallel to the marked 'roll' lines. It is important that the panels run at right angles to the leech so the strong fill threads take the high leech load.

Once the cloth is pinned in position, the broadseam is drawn onto the top edge of each panel by running a pencil along the lower raised edge of the tape on the pattern. The sail cutter then runs his scissors along the other side of the tape to trim off the excess cloth.

The bottom edge of the adjacent panel is left straight, so that when the two are seamed together shape is forced into the sail. Batten pockets are drawn on in a similar fashion. The ends of the battens serve to mark the leech position and should be arranged to accommodate the maximum girth measurements (across the sail) allowed by the class rules. The luff curve is usually drawn on as a series of marks on each panel which are later faired through once the panels have been sewn together.

Below and right: Making a sail. (1) The Mylar pattern has raised tapes to define the shapes of the broadseams, leech and luff, and the positions of the battens. (2) The curve of the broadseam is vital. Here the shape has been modified by adding a leech take-up. (3) The cloth is carefully pinned and then rolled out across the pattern at right angles to the leech.

1

2

3

4

5

Above: (4) The broadseam is transferred to the cloth by
running a pencil down the lower edge of the raised tape. (5)
The panel is cut by guiding the scissors along the upper edge
of the tape. This gives a curved panel with a 15mm allowance
for the seam.

Below: (6) Double-sided tape is stuck along the pencil line.
(7) The straight (uncut) edge of the next panel is stuck down
carefully along the pencil line. This puts curve into the sail.

6

7

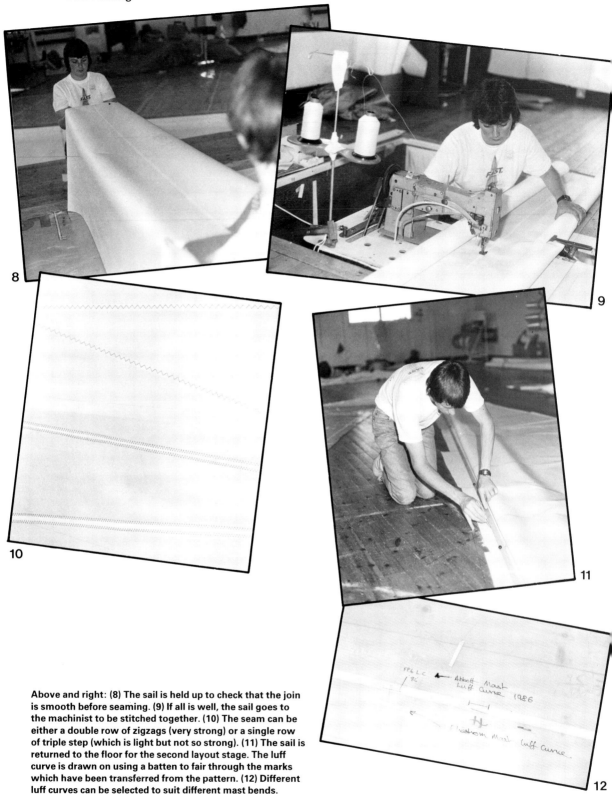

Above and right: (8) The sail is held up to check that the join is smooth before seaming. (9) If all is well, the sail goes to the machinist to be stitched together. (10) The seam can be either a double row of zigzags (very strong) or a single row of triple step (which is light but not so strong). (11) The sail is returned to the floor for the second layout stage. The luff curve is drawn on using a batten to fair through the marks which have been transferred from the pattern. (12) Different luff curves can be selected to suit different mast bends.

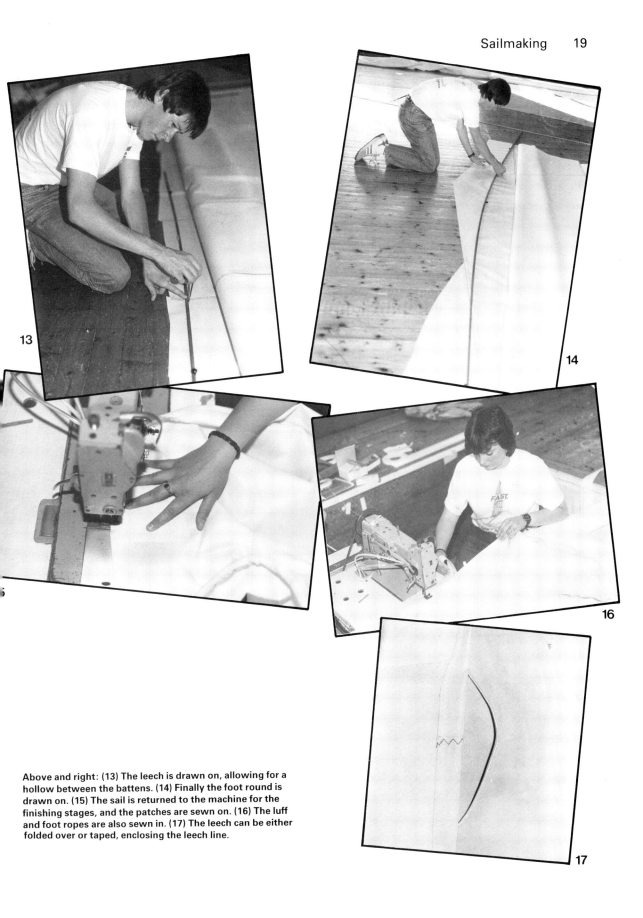

Above and right: (13) The leech is drawn on, allowing for a hollow between the battens. (14) Finally the foot round is drawn on. (15) The sail is returned to the machine for the finishing stages, and the patches are sewn on. (16) The luff and foot ropes are also sewn in. (17) The leech can be either folded over or taped, enclosing the leech line.

Recording the shape

The object of using a full-size pattern (rather than a list of offsets from a straight line) is to reproduce exactly the same sail shape every time. Drawn carefully, the broadseam should be accurate to within the width of a pencil line. The other great advantage of the full-size pattern is that it provides a record of several different luff curves.

It is worth ensuring that your sailmaker records any new design he may develop with you in this way, so that if it proves fast you can order the same shape again and be confident of getting it. Sail shape is very dependent upon the form of the broadseam: while there may be the same amount of broadseam in each panel, (measured as an offset from a straight line), the result can be very different, depending how the batten is faired through the points. Consequently sails which are hand-lofted from a series of offsets seldom come out the same twice.

Above: As an alternative to using the Mylar pattern, computer-designed sails are often cut direct from the computer program by a table plotter.

Computer cutting

An alternative method of cutting has been developed in the last few years, using computer-driven plotter tables. Computer cutting is a natural progression from computer designing or 'moulding' of sails, and removes the need for any Mylar patterns.

The sail is first created as a three-dimensional mould shape which is described numerically, but can also be viewed graphically on a VDU screen. The computer program then drapes cloth around the mould in any chosen fashion, with horizontal, vertical or radial panels, and calculates the broadseam necessary in each panel to achieve the designed shape. This information is then transferred directly to the table plotter which automatically cuts each panel of the sail. As the plotter arm moves up and down the table a suspended pen draws the seam line; a laser or high-speed cutting disc then trims a seam width outside the line. The cut panels are then ready for seaming. (An added advantage of describing sails numerically is that they can be transmitted around the world via telex or on floppy disc).

Whichever system of cutting sails your sailmaker uses, it is essential that it is accurate and reproduceable. The beauty of the computer design and cutting system is that a sail shape can be modified on the computer screen and then cut straight away without having to alter any templates. The computer-cut sail is fully described numerically, which allows shapes to be compared quantitatively. Depth, draft and twist measurements from photographs of the flying sail

can also be compared directly with the original design to check how closely the two correspond. A computer-cut sail is theoretically more accurate than one cut by hand as the variable human element is removed. However, in practice the smoothness of the sail will always depend on how well the panels are put together.

Gluing and seaming

Before seaming, the panels are carefully stuck together with double-sided sticky tape so there is no danger of the seam moving apart while it is being sewn. The straight bottom edge of one panel is glued down with double-sided tape along the pencil line drawn on the top edge of the adjacent panel. In fact the sticky tape contributes greatly to the strength of the seam, and is so strong that it is possible to stick several panels together and then hold them up before sewing to check that each seam is smooth. If there are any bumps, the seam can be pulled apart and restuck several times until the sailmaker is happy.

With yarn-tempered cloth, any wrinkle in the seam causes a major lump which stretches a long way into the panel, so any deviation from the fair curve of the broadseam line is magnified several times. The preliminary taping of the seams makes this much less likely during the actual operation of sewing the panels, as although the needle line may wander a little, the seam will not.

Stitching

The type of stitch used is dictated by the amount of loading placed on the seam, but for most one-design sails a triple-step seam is used. For higher-load applications, a double row of zig-zag stitches provides a slightly stronger seam, and is more resistant to wear.

The correct choice of thread weight, stitch tension and seam width is vital in order to achieve a smooth but strong seam. When seaming laminated fabrics, there is a tendency for the Mylar film to tear slightly around the needle holes as tension is applied to the seam. To prevent this 'seam creep', a sticky Dacron tape is applied to the seam on the shiny, Mylar side of the fabric before sewing. In the early days of Mylar sails, all seams were taped in this way, but with improvements in both fabrics and seaming techniques, seams are now only taped in high-load areas, mainly around the clew.

THE LAYOUT STAGE

Once all the panels are seamed together, with the batten pockets and windows sewn on, the sail returns to the floor to be layed out.

Luff curve

Matching the luff curve on the sail to the exact amount of mast bend in your rig is one of the most important factors in achieving correct sail shape. The sailmaker often has several luff curves marked on his pattern for the popular mast sections in use within the class. However, if you are using a new or different mast section, or if your rig set-up or crew weight demands that your mast bends differently from others, you will have to tell the sailmaker so that he may make the necessary modifications.

The luff curve is drawn onto the sail by pinning a batten along the marks from the Mylar pattern. The secret of obtaining a smooth and fair curve is

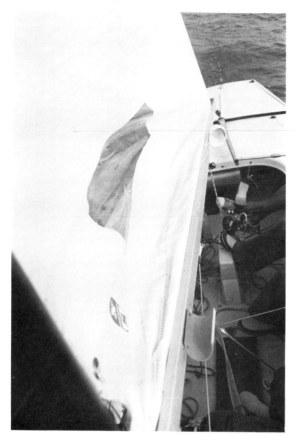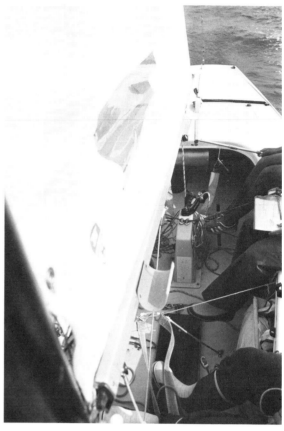

Above: The lensfoot is controlled by the outhaul. On the left the outhaul is off; on the right the outhaul is on.

a combination of a good pattern and an experienced sailmaker who can 'tweak' the batten to match the mast bend.

Trimming the leech

At layout, the position of the leech is already defined by the batten pocket ends and the head and clew. However, it is not simply a question of joining up the points with straight lines. In order to minimise leech flutter a certain amount of hollow is cut into the leech between each batten to keep the trailing edge under tension. The right amount of hollow is critical. Too much and the leech will not open easily, too little and it will flutter readily between battens. In the case of a jib, considerably more hollow is cut into the sail to prevent flutter, as a sail without battens is unable to support any degree of roach (roach is any area of sail behind a straight line from head to clew).

The leech of a mainsail may be finished off by folding over the cloth, or by trimming along the leech and sewing a folded tape over the edge. On a jib, folding the leech over tends to cause it to hook up; it is therefore normally finished with the lightest possible tape. The leech tape must be sewn on with a very loose tension, as if the stitch is at all tight, this too will cause the leech to hook up. For this reason some sailmakers simply hot knife the jib leech, although eventually the edge will begin to fray.

It is well worth having a leech line fitted to a large genoa as it can considerably extend the sail's life. All genoas will tend to flutter or vibrate on the leech as the breeze gets up, and if this is allowed to happen the cloth right on the edge of the sail will soon break down completely. Once this occurs the sail will begin to flutter in lower wind strengths and will soon become a major

problem. If a leech line is fitted, all that is needed is a little tension on the line to stop the fluttering completely.

Any genoa that is the size of a 505 or International 14 or larger will benefit from having a leech line fitted. A neat method of securing the tail of the line is inside a Velcro pocket. With this system the tab is adjustable; it does not catch on the shrouds and there are no loose ends to get wrapped around the rigging.

The foot

The foot is the last edge of the sail to be laid out. The jib foot is finished in a similar way to the leech with a light tape and often a foot line. Usually the sailmaker will opt for the maximum foot round allowed by the class rules so that the bottom of the headsail just touches the deck to minimise air flow under the sail. Many of the new one design classes now favour a loose footed arrangement for the mainsail to gain greater projected area downwind and to cut out the need for a track on the boom. Older designs still use the stretchy shelf foot with a sewn-in elastic boltrope. Once around the windward mark the outhaul can be eased off, the clew slides inboard of its own accord and the shelf helps to ensure the mainsail takes up the correct horizontal camber directly above the boom.

Jib luff systems

The use of rod rigging and no jib halyard is now popular on many performance dinghies that need high rig tension. If you are using a rod forestay the jib luff tube must be wide enough to slide over the end terminal fitting. At the head a short webbing loop is sufficient to lash the sail to the jib strop. Luff tension can be applied by simply tying the tack down to the bow fitting or, if class rules permit, made adjustable with a small cleat sewn onto the luff. The other common luff system is a stainless steel wire sewn into the luff tube with swaged eyes tied to the head and tack rings in the sail. Ask for Dyform wire, which has less crimp due to the interlocking nature of the strands and so stretches less than conventional 1 x 19 wire.

Keelboat and sportsboat jibs often have no luff wire, just a heavy tape hanked onto the forestay or a zipper. With these systems it is simple to control the draft position by altering luff tension via the jib halyard.

Handwork

The final stage in building a sail is to fit the hardware: headboard, press rings, leech line

Above: This radial patch is designed to hold the middle of the sail flat while allowing the leech to twist open.

cleat and clew slug. The luff rope and foot ropes (if fitted) are tensioned to give some elasticity: this makes the sail more responsive to halyard and outhaul control. Finally the numbers and telltales are attached and the sail is ready for action.

Latest developments in sailmaking

In the last few years the main developments in sailmaking have been towards engineering the sail with few or no seams at all and reducing the overall weight.

Every time a stitched seam crosses a load line it causes stretch as the needle holes become elongated under load and allow movement. In fact with laminated fabrics the needle holes can cause the Mylar film to tear if there is no polyester substrate bonded to it. This is why the early Mylar sails all had sticky Dacron tape applied over all the seam lines. Today most of the major sail lofts have the technology to glue seams together without the need for sewing, thus

avoiding the main cause of sail stretch. The full benefit of high modulus fabrics such as Kevlar, Spectra, Carbon fibre and P.B.O. Zylon (an isotopic liquid crystal polymer) is that these high performance fibres are not compromised by seam stretch and can be used continuously from head to clew and can provide considerable weight savings for the same if not greater strength. The fabrics can also be constructed with fewer woven fibres if no seam stitching is required. Some of the most obvious examples of this are the "Tapedrive" sails built from 52 inch (1320 mm) shaped Mylar panels, stuck together, over which continuous Kevlar or Polyester tapes are laid down from head to clew, following the predicted stress lines in the sail. The Mylar is there as a membrane to hold the load bearing tapes in place and to stop the air blowing through and is not intended to contribute to the strength of the sail. These light-weight sails do seem to respond well to picking up the lightest zephyrs and hold their shape well when softer and heavier fabrics hang down

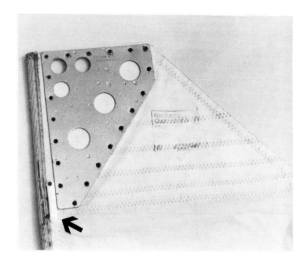

Above: Note the slug (arrowed) on this Finn headboard, which holds the headboard at the correct angle to the mast and tightens the leech.

shapelessly in light airs but may not take so kindly to constant abuse and flexing after a season of heavy conditions (unless a more flexible substrate is used as the carrier film).

Moulded 'membrane' sails

In an effort to produce the 'ultimate' light and low stretch sail, a system has been developed over the last ten years to build 'moulded' sails right from their basic components. In effect the sailmaker is making sailcloth: creating the laminate as the sail is built up from the Mylar substrate film, gluing on the load-bearing fibres exactly as and where they are required (Polyester, Mylar, Spectra, Kevlar, carbon, PBO, whatever), finishing with a final layer of bonded Mylar.

Panelled sails

But many sailmaking companies prefer to stay with sails which are designed and cut by computer, built from a variety of fabric weights and styles to match the loads in the sail and arranged in tri-radial panels, as shown on pages 63 & 73. They question if loads in the sail do actually travel neatly along individual fibres or tapes and argue that this static model changes as soon as sail controls are applied, the mast bends or a gust strikes. While their rejection of the new technology may be based on their not having access to it, there are now commercially-available

glue guns which allow even the smallest of local sail lofts to glue their seams. However, when gluing laminates together there is little seam strength advantage to be gained from gluing the surface Mylar films together because the main loads are carried by the fibres in the fabric underneath and it is this part of the laminate that needs to be glued to avoid stretch. The only way to improve on the stitched seam is to layer the joint, glue fibre to fibre and then film to film, which is difficult with fabric off a roll. But the panelled sailmakers do perhaps have a greater degree of freedom to place the position and the amount of shape in the sail.

Panelled sails are now being produced using the full benefit of the raw materials developed specifically for sailcloth. Two examples are the new Kevlar Edge Fibre (which retains more of its strength when folded) and Magnashield film (which protects the fibres from the degrading effect of sunlight). Hyde Sails has developed its own custom material which incorporates both of these.

Above: A tape luff secured by poppers around the forestay. This is a common arrangement on keelboats.

One of the main limitations of moulded sails is that they don't handle off-the-thread-line loads, which occur when a sail flogs or when it's loaded from clew to luff when the mast over-bends. The new Hyde material copes with these loads by incorporating two Spectra x-ply layers (laminated at six and twelve degrees off the thread line) and a Vectran rip stop fill. All of these materials add to the strength and durability of the sailcloth and now make Kevlar sails a viable option for many sailors.

3 Planning your campaign

Assuming you are beginning a campaign in a new class, how do you go about choosing the fastest combination of sails and spars for your new boat? The best starting point is a visit to the Nationals or some other major championships, armed with a camera and a note book. Aim to compile a complete list of the equipment used by the top ten boats. Your list should include columns for the make of the hull, mast, mainsail, jib and spinnaker.

Check the boats in the dinghy park yourself to find exactly which mast sections and mainsails were used: don't rely on hearsay, which is invariably out of date. To do your homework properly, you need to find out not only which mast section was used but the length of the taper; whether the top section was pressed or internally or externally sleeved, and where. At one world championship, there were three versions of the same mast section in use within the top ten boats. Similarly with sails, you should note which sailmaker was used for each sail, and which design. Had the luff curve been modified, or had other changes been made from the original pattern?

Below left and right: Find out which are the top boats and take photos like these to get an idea of the amount of jib luff sag, mast rake and mast bend they use.

Rig shots

If you can manage to get on the water during your regatta visit, any photos of boats sailing upwind, from abeam and head on, will give you an indication of the current range of mast rake in the class, and how straight the masts are held sideways. Take as many photos as you can to help you make your choice of rig.

Many dinghy classes are not as one-design as you think, and permit quite a range of rig options, such as the use of diamonds on a Contender, a high or low jib box on a 505, single or double spreaders on an International 14.

When taking photos of the boats' layout, you should also note whether spinnaker bags or chutes are more popular and which system is easiest and fastest to use. In the case of the Fireball, the benefits stack up in favour of the bag system as the spinnaker is relatively small and quick to douse, and the boat remains a lot drier downwind without the chute.

However, on an International 14 the spinnaker is a lot larger and would take forever to stuff into a bag. Since the boats are undecked, there is little to gain from not using a chute.

The more regattas you can repeat this procedure for, the more consistent a picture you can build up of the performance of each item of equipment. For the less obvious details, such as the exact model name of a sail, you will have to ask the crew themselves. If this information is unforthcoming, a call to the supplier should provide all the answers you require.

Below: Hang up a jib like this to assess the shape.

Choosing a sailmaker

How far you pursue your research will depend on your own level of competition. If you are mainly involved in club racing, the standard version of the championship-winning rig will be fine. But if you are beginning an international or Olympic campaign, you may wish to start off by duplicating the current champions' equipment exactly.

By using the same rig as the fastest boats, you will have a 'boat speed benchmark' to work towards. When you feel that you are of a sufficient standard to develop new sails, your objective will be to surpass this benchmark, and you must choose a sailmaker who can help you do this. Apart from a proven reputation in the class and a good database of previous designs, he must:
- be active and interested in your class;
- be easily accessible to you;
- have something special to offer, such as high quality fabrics or 'hi-tech' constructions;
- be helpful and easy to work with.

The current market leader may not always be interested in updating his designs if they are already selling well. On the other hand, think carefully before working with a sail loft with no previous experience in your class, as the sailmaker may end up learning at your expense.

WHAT YOUR SAILMAKER NEEDS TO KNOW

For the majority of dinghy and keelboat sails the sailmakers' specification will be fairly complete, but he will still have several questions for you.

General sailing conditions

Some sailmakers produce different sail shapes for inland and coastal conditions. If most of your sailing is on flat inland waters, ask the sailmaker to ensure that your sails have a fine entry to the luff, for optimum pointing ability.

Mast section

The choice of mast affects the shape of the luff curve, and the use of an uncommon luff system may involve fitting a non-standard boltrope. Always advise the sailmaker which brand of spar you will be using. You should also advise how the mast is to be rigged:

- single or double spreaders;
- lower shrouds or not;
- height of trapeze wires;
- whether a strut or mast ram is to be used.

All these details decide the shape of the luff curve and help the sailmaker match the sail to the spar.

Crew weight

If the crew weight is particularly light or heavy you should tell the sailmaker. A big discrepancy from the norm will require the mast to be bent relatively more or less, and the luff curve will have to be altered to accommodate the difference.

Jib luff systems

Depending on the class rules, you may have a choice of jib luff system. If you are sailing a J24, you have a choice between the headfoil system or snap poppers. Using the poppers has the advantage of not needing a man on the foredeck to re-hoist the sail, but it is a lot slower than the headfoil when you come to change sails. The Dragon is one of the keelboat classes which allow a zipper luff; this totally encloses the forestay and allows for rapid sail changes.

The rules for many classes dictate that the luff wire shall be fixed at both ends, which means using the conventional luff wire system lashed at the head.

Windows

Crash, collision or vision windows are very useful when you are attempting to line up on a hectic start line, but sailors often worry that putting a window in the sail will affect the cloth stretch in that area. Fitted correctly, windows should make very little difference to the sail shape, as they are generally positioned in low-load areas near the luff or foot. Nevertheless, avoid asking for windows in the luff of heavy air jibs, as used on the J24 or Soling; these are subject to high halyard loadings, and some local distortion above the window may result.

Some regatta sailors of boats with large genoas also fit a 'pre-start window' below the collision window near the foot, so that when the sail is flying high and loose before the start, vision is not reduced at the critical moment.

If permitted, another useful window can be incorporated in the luff of the mainsail just below the spreaders. Positioned correctly, this spreader window provides the crew with a ready visual guide as to how far in the headsail leech is trimmed against the reference point of the spreaders. This is particularly useful on trapeze dinghies and keelboats, where boatspeed is sacrificed by climbing down from the high side to look under the boom and check the jib sheeting.

Special fittings

Most boats have one or two non-standard fittings which may require minor changes to the cut of the sail.

One critical measurement to check is the knock-back at the tack of the mainsail. This is the distance from the aft side of the mast to the tack pin. If the amount of knock-back does not fit your spars, the sail will always set with a crease. Too much is better than too little, as an extra shackle can easily be added to give a smooth fit. Alternatively,

Left: Collision window in the jib and main. Above: A spreader window in the main. This helps the crew on the windward side check the genoa sheeting in relation to the spreader.

a simple lashing provides an easily adjustable solution.

For boats using a stuff luff system on the jib, some system is required for tensioning the luff. A small cleat mounted by the tack is one option, allowing adjustment on the water.

If your boat has a spinnaker chute you will need a retrieval patch on the sail, or possibly two if it is a large sail in a short chute. Some keelboat sailors use a swivel shackle on the spinnaker head and Englefield clips taped onto the clew rings. Launching a spinnaker from the cockpit in a Soling or Dragon is made easier by folding the sail into a tight bundle, secured by a Velcro tab. When needed the sail is thrown out of the cockpit in the bundle; by striking the sheet and guy when the sail is half hoisted, the sail sets straight away and well clear of the rig.

Below and right: Measuring mast pre-bend against a straight string stretched between the black bands.

Development classes

If you sail a development class you will have many more options to discuss with the sailmaker. Most sail lofts will have developed a preferred specification for such boats, including a recommended sail area distribution for main and jib. Minor variations from the sailmaker's standard dimensions can be accommodated without problem, but if you ask him to change his sail area ratios dramatically, then you will be moving away from the carefully developed and proven sail shapes.

However, whichever class you sail, it is well worth reading the class rules to check out the full range of rig options allowed. You may find, for example, that the jib is only limited to a maximum

sail area, in which case you could have a tall, thin sail or a short, wide one.

The tall, thin jib is definitely faster upwind, especially on flat water, but downwind in choppy conditions a lower-aspect sail is quicker in marginal planing conditions. This may well be because the lower-aspect sail is easier to set and read offwind.

So if you mainly race inland try using a high-aspect sail, but if you are sailing in a regatta circuit of predominantly coastal venues you may decide to opt for the more conventional lower-aspect sail.

WHAT THE SAILMAKER SHOULD TELL YOU

Many sailmakers issue a tuning leaflet with their sails with basic guidelines for setting up the rig. The tuning guide should provide you with the following information to coarse-tune the rig.

Below and right: Measuring mast rake: log the distance from the upper black band to the top of the transom (or to the intersection between the transom and the floor).

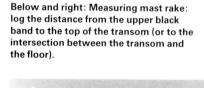

Mast pre-bend

The amount of pre-bend which the mainsail luff is cut to fit is measured with rig tension applied but without the sail rigged. The reading is taken at spreader height from the aft side of the mast to a straight string stretched from black band to black band. The mast is pre-bent either by angling the spreaders aft, increasing their length or increasing rig tension.

Rake

The degree of fore and aft rake suited to the sails is commonly measured by hoisting a tape to the head of the mast on the main halyard, and measuring off at the intersection of the deck and the transom, or hull and transom.

Forestay tension

Forestay tension controls the amount of leeward forestay sag which in turn affects pointing ability. The sailmaker cuts the jib's luff hollow to accommodate a certain degree of forestay sag and it is vital to set the boat up with a corresponding rig tension. This is best measured using a tension meter.

Spreader length

Your sailmaker should give you guide to spreader length and deflection, which will provide a useful starting point for setting up the rig. Your crew weight will determine whether you then shorten or lengthen them. In general, the longer the spreaders the stiffer the mast will be held sideways. However, if the spreaders are too long the leech will not open up when you're overpowered, and the mast will be pushed to leeward and pump sideways in a strong breeze.*

WHICH SAILS?

The size of your sail inventory will depend on the size of your boat and your budget, and the range of conditions you are likely to encounter. For most dinghy classes the sails are all-purpose and choice is a question of which design or make. With keelboats you are often faced with a choice of light, heavy or all-purpose sails for both main and jib. This can create a dilemma when you are allowed to measure in only two of each at a regatta.

Below and below right: Measuring the rig tension. Using a tension meter, pull the pointer to the mark and then read where the centre of the shroud cuts the scale. Finally use the chart on the back of the meter to convert to kilograms or pounds. In this case the tension is 255 kg (560lb).

For example, consider the options if you race a Dragon.

Club Racing:
●   General purpose mainsail, 0 – 25 knots.
●   Medium/heavy genoa, 8 – 25 knots, with fine entry for optimum pointing ability.
●   All-purpose tri-radial spinnaker.

Club racing and open events:
●   General purpose mainsail.
●   Flat, medium/heavy genoa.
●   Full, medium/heavy genoa, for choppy sea conditions.
●   Optional light-air genoa, 0 – 12 knots.
●   All-purpose tri-radial spinnaker.

International regatta circuit:
●   General purpose mainsail.
●   Heavy-air mainsail, 23 knots plus.
●   Light-air genoa, 0 – 12 knots.
●   Flat medium/heavy genoa.
●   Full medium/heavy genoa.
●   Tri-radial reaching spinnaker.
●   Running spinnaker.

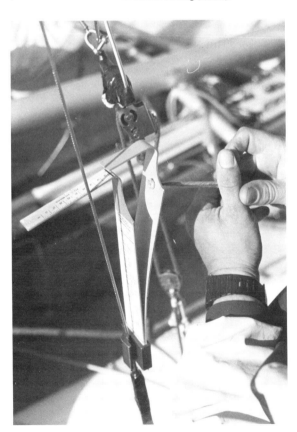
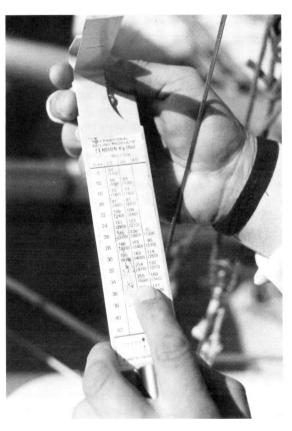

Mylar or Dacron

Mylar is often the best fabric for building headsails, but it is not always ideal for dinghy mainsails, where a certain amount of stretch is generally required. Where Mylar does score over Dacron is in the greater range of panel constructions it permits. Compared to Dacron, there is a much larger range of 'warp orientated' fabrics available (fabrics strongest in the long, warp direction) in Mylar. This means that it is often possible to build radial Mylar sails which could not be cut from Dacron as no suitable warp cloth is available.

Properly looked after a Mylar sail should last a little longer than a yarn-tempered sail. Where a Dacron sail will stretch a little every time it is hoisted, but retain some elasticity, a Mylar sail will stretch very little until it reaches the point at which the fabric is overloaded. Thereafter, the Mylar permanently deforms and the sail suddenly becomes uncompetitive. This is why you will often see a maximum windspeed stamped on the clew of a Mylar genoa. As long as the sailmaker selects the correct cloth weight for a given windspeed and the owner takes care not to exceed that range, a Mylar sail should enjoy a long life.

Below: Measuring spreader deflection: put a straight edge across the spreader tips and measure from it to the back of the mast.

Radial constructions

Radial panel constructions are a very strong method of engineering a sail. Radial panels have become the standard configuration on offshore boats in recent years, and they are now increasingly common among the one-design classes.

The first steps towards building radial sails were made during the 12-metre campaigns of 1983. Computer-generated stress maps showed that a sail's maximum loading was in the leech area, travelling in an arc between head and clew. By referring to such stress maps sailmakers were able to align warp-orientated fabrics with the sail loading; the result was the radial configuration.

Above: The maximum wind speed for this Mylar genoa is 22 knots.

The radial panels originate from the head and clew. They are joined by horizontal seams wherever a change of warp direction is required to keep the warp line parallel to the load line.

The vertical leech panels dramatically reduce leech stretch, while the overall arrangement allows the clew loads to follow the warp threads in the fabric as they spread into the sail.

As the radial construction results in a stronger sail the cloth weight can be relatively lighter than a conventional cross-cut sail. The reinforcement patches can also be reduced, resulting in a lighter all up weight which allows the sail to tack faster and set more easily in lighter airs.

See Tuning your Dinghy, Lawrie Smith, Fernhurst Books.

4 Sail setting

Sail setting is a two-stage process: fitting the sails to the boat, and setting them up using the sail shaping controls.

FITTING

When you try the sails on the boat for the first time, it is important to check their dimensions. The mainsail should set between the black bands on mast and boom when the halyard and outhaul are fully tensioned. If the sail appears short in the foot or luff, ease the tension in the sewn-in bolt rope. Tensioned too tightly the bolt rope can

Right: Lashing the tack cringle carefully allows the sail to set without creases. Below and below right: This Finn takes the idea further; an adjustable inhaul effectively alters the shape of the luff curve in the lower third of the sail. Pulling the tack forward adds luff curve.

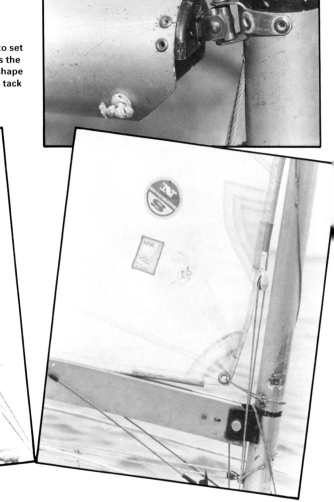

prevent the sails from being pulled out to the bands. Don't worry if the jib luff measures close to the minimum: headsails are often laid out to the minimum luff but maximum leech length in order to get the clew as low as possible, so enhancing the end plate effect.

Fixing the tack

Tie or pin the mainsail tack in position with the right amount of knock-back, so that the sail sets without creases.

Shackle the headsail onto the forward part of the bow fitting at a height that allows the foot to sweep the deck. If your boat is fitted with tack horns, as on the J24, you need to ignore them and attach the tack ring to a central shackle. This arrangement allows the sail to set in the same lead position on both tacks, whereas using the tack horns involves different sheeting positions for each side of the boat.

Battens

When fitting the battens, ensure that the ends push back hard against the leech. Check they are fully captive within their pockets and not just caught inside the leech tape.

Boats with a full-length top batten (one that butts up against the mast) such as the 420, 470 and 505, will require a stiff batten for heavy air and a softer one of around 3.5lbs (1.5kg) compression for medium conditions. It may also be necessary to vary the stiffness of the tapered battens lower down the sail. In a strong breeze the bottom two battens need to be stiff in order to hold the leech straight and flat, and to prevent the sail from inverting.

The lightest battens are of the foam-cored variety; sleeved in glass on two sides. These battens tend to develop their maximum bend at 30% aft of the tip, rather further forward than usual; this allows more fullness to be carried in the head of the sail in medium conditions.

If the inboard end of the batten creates local creases in the sail, try replacing the end caps with tape.

SAIL CONTROLS

When you are satisfied that the sails are properly fitted, you can begin setting them up using the various controls.

Mastbend

Mastbend is the main device used for setting the amount of fullness in the mainsail and controlling the degree of forestay tension.

The mast should be set up with a prescribed degree of pre-bend to match the luff curve the sailmaker has put into the sail, but further pre-bending by rig tension is necessary when there is insufficient wind to cause the mast to bend naturally and achieve the designed depth, draft and leech shape.

As the breeze gets up, bend the mast more than the initial pre-bend by a) removing the chocks in front of the mast; b) angling the spreader tips aft; c) increasing the rig tension. This will serve to flatten out the top two-thirds of the sail by increasing the distance from leech to luff. (On the other hand a dead straight mast will give you the deepest, most powerful sail shape.) Bending the mast also loosens off the leech, because the distance from mast tip to clew has been decreased. The draft position will tend to move aft as the sail is flattened off.

Left: Adjust the height of the jib tack so the foot of the sail sweeps the deck.

35%

42.5%

45%

Above: The effect of luff tension on a Soling jib. (Left) halyard too tight – draft 35%. (Right) perfect – draft 42.5%. (Centre) halyard too loose – draft 45%.

Luff tension

A sail's draft position (the point of maximum depth) is controlled by the amount of tension on the luff. As more tension is applied to the luff, the draft point moves forward, from around 50% when completely slack to 30 – 35% aft of the leading edge when full on.

Many sailors get this the wrong way round, believing that the harder they pull the halyard the flatter the front of the sail will become. To convince yourself that the draft really does move forward, try repeatedly hauling on luff tension and then letting it go; you will soon see the way the maximum depth slides forward and back in the sail. The best way to observe this is to lie in the boat and look up the mainsail from underneath the boom while someone else pumps the halyard a few times. Try to picture the depth and draft position in percentage terms. Once you have determined where the draft position is in the sail, you should become familiar with locating it from your normal sailing position.

Below: The cunningham pulls the draft forward in the main. A secondary effect is to open the top of the leech. (Left) cunningham on. (Right) cunningham off.

In practice mainsail luff tension is controlled by a combination of the halyard and the cunningham, which can be thought of as an additional tensioning device for use once the sail has been pulled up to the black bands, and which allows easy adjustment for upwind and downwind legs. Most dinghies use wire halyards to reduce stretch, which hook onto a rack, highfield lever or muscle-box. These systems provide for basic light or heavy air settings, while the cunningham provides the fine tune.

A greater range of luff tension is often required on keelboats, and this is governed by how tight the halyard is set. Most boats of this size use a small winch to wind up the tension. When running downwind in light airs, for example, it is common practice to ease the mainsail down the mast a few inches to produce a smoother and fuller shape near the luff.

The role of the cunningham

As the breeze gets up and the mainsail is stretched out to the black bands, the draft will move aft to around 55% as a result of the increased loading on the sailcloth. With the draft in this position the

Below and below left: The effect of the clew outhaul. (Left) outhaul eased – note the curve in the foot of the sail and the closed leech in this area. (Right) tensioning the outhaul has the opposite effect.

sail is very prone to stall and provides little power in a chop. It is the job of the cunningham to pull the draft back to its designed position: around 44% back from the luff.

An important secondary action of the cunningham is to free off the upper leech, depowering the sail, which in turn reduces the amount of weather helm.

Outhaul

The outhaul is used to set the required amount of depth in the lower third of the mainsail. This varies with the amount of breeze, and is altered for upwind and downwind legs. A particularly efficient outhaul system for trapeze boats incorporates a lever set under the boom for throwing off a fixed amount of outhaul for the reach, but also includes a clam cleat for fine adjustment of the upwind position. The crew has only a few seconds inside the boat when tacking and it is much faster to simply knock off a lever than it is to ease a line out through a cleat. If the foot rope is elasticated the clew will move forward of its own accord when released, opening up the shelf foot to give a full reaching shape.

The outhaul also has an effect on lower leech tension. Easing the clew firms up the leech below the bottom batten quite significantly.

Mainsheet

The mainsheet controls the amount of twist in the leech. A closed or tight leech is one with little twist, with the top batten parallel to the end of the boom. Easing the mainsheet allows the boom to rise up and puts more twist into the top of the sail. This open leech allows the air to escape more freely from the top of the sail, creating less drag and less sideways force.

Main traveller

The traveller is used to position the boom relative to the centreline of the boat. As such the traveller is closely involved with mainsheet tension and the

Right: The effect of the mainsheet. (Top) tight mainsheet reduces twist and improves pointing. (Right) easing the mainsheet a few centimetres twists off the leech for extra power in light airs and depowers the sail in heavy airs.

action of the two controls should be considered together. The traveller has direct control over the size of the jib slot and the amount of weather helm. The traveller is eased to leeward with increasing wind strength in order to reduce weather helm. As a result, the slot between main and jib is reduced and the jib lead has to be moved outboard to compensate.

Kicking strap (vang)

The kicking strap or vang is used to bend the mast low down by forcing the boom forwards at the gooseneck, and is used to help flatten off the sail in heavy air. The vang can also be used instead of the mainsheet to set up the leech tension in strong winds, while the mainsheet is constantly used to adjust the angle of the boom. This technique is known as 'vang-sheeting' and is common practice among Laser sailors.

Downwind the vang is used to control the amount of twist in the main and prevents the top of the sail being blown forward of the mast.

Forestay tension

Forestay tension controls:
- The amount of fullness in the jib.
- The degree of pointing ability.

The forestay can sag off an enormous amount to leeward while sailing. This sag puts extra fullness into the jib, over and above that already cut into the sail; the result is that the boat loses pointing ability owing to the jib becoming very draft forward.

In practice, most high-performance dinghies such as the 470 use considerable forestay tension throughout most of the wind range because the hull is light and easily driven and a lack of pointing ability would be disastrous. However, heavier keelboats such as the Soling and Dragon require extra power in the front of the headsail in light winds, so it is usual to allow the forestay to sag several inches in these condtions.

Above: Jib luff sag, one of the main speed controls on a Soling, is to be avoided on most dinghies.

Below: Setting up the jib luff tension (see text).

Jib luff tension

In the case of dinghy jibs the degree of luff tension is determined by how tightly the head cringle is lashed to the eye of the luff wire. Some class rules permit stuff luffs and a jib cunningham which allow the tension to be altered while sailing.

To set the jib luff tension string up the sail

Top: Loosening the jib halyard on a Soling allows the flow to move aft and opens the leech.
Above: Tightening the halyard has the opposite effect, and can be used to completely close the top leech of the jib.

horizontally between two posts with the tension on the luff wire which you would use while sailing. With the tack eye fixed to the luff wire apply sufficient tension to the head of the sail to virtually remove the creases at the luff. This is your flat water, optimum pointing set-up. Tightening the head lashing even more pulls the draft further forward for power in choppy conditions where pointing ability is less important.

Keelboat headsails generally use a stretchy rope or a heavy luff tape, which allows the draft position to be determined directly via halyard tension. Tightening the luff pulls the head further away from the foot, which also tensions the leech. A few inches of halyard tension can completely close the top leech of a Dragon or Soling headsail. Any adjustment to the halyard should be accompanied by moving the jib leads upwards to maintain the original leech tension.

Jib sheeting position

The best advice on jib sheeting is to use a system which, while remaining within the the class rules, allows you the widest range of lead positions. The systems permitted by the rules may range from the fixed fairleads found on the Cadet to the athwartships travellers with barber haulers common on the Dragon.

Moving the jib leads fore and aft has a similar effect to sliding them up and down vertically. Moving the lead forward places more of the sheet

Below: The effect of the barber hauler. (Left) a loose barber hauler opens the jib leech. (Centre) as the barber hauler is pulled down the leech becomes tighter. (Right) a tight barber hauler produces a tight leech.

tension down the leech and less along the foot. This is a good starting point for medium airs, when a firm leech is required for good pointing ability, and when there is no danger of the mainsail being backwinded, because the boom is on the centreline.

As the breeze gets up the jib lead is pulled progressively aft, in order to flatten off the lower part of the sail and to free off the top of the leech. The open leech allows:
- The air to escape more freely from the sail.
- An increase in the size of the slot, allowing the main traveller to be eased down to leeward to balance the increasing weather helm experienced in a strong breeze.
- The boat to be sailed more upright as heeling forces are reduced.

When finding the correct jib lead position for a particular wind strength the telltales provide a useful rule of thumb. Luff gently just above close hauled, so that the windward telltales begin to lift. If the top telltale lifts before the bottom one, the lead is too far aft and needs to be moved forward or down. Conversely, move the leads aft or up if the bottom telltale lifts first. When all the telltales lift at the same moment the jib luff is at the same angle of incidence to the wind from head to tack and is trimmed perfectly.

Sheeting angles

When people talk about sheeting angles they are referring to the angle the jibsheet makes with the centre line. The optimum angle for good pointing is around eight degrees but depends on the hull shape and headsail size.

A non-overlapping jib can be sheeted much closer than a large genoa without causing the main to backwind.

The basic rule is to sheet as far inboard as possible without causing the sail to stall; this gives the best pointing ability. As the wind increases and the waves get up the tendency to stall increases and the jib has to be sheeted at a wider angle; this provides more speed at the expense of pointing and is known as 'footing'.

It is important to have as much control over the sheeting angle as the class rules permit. In the Cadet and 420 classes where the jib lead is fixed at a very wide angle the trick is to barber-haul the sheet closer in by pulling on the windward sheet. If you are allowed athwartships tracks fit them. However, if you wish to keep the layout simple use a single fore-and-aft track which is angled outwards at the back. Then as the lead is moved aft for heavy air the slot is opened up automatically.

SETTING UP THE SAILS

Having looked at each of the sail shaping controls and how they work, it is time to consider how to set up the sails for beating in medium wind conditions. The following directions may not apply exactly to your particular boat or rig, but should serve as a useful starting point for correct trim.

Mainsail

1   Set up the mast with the prescribed pre-bend using rig tension, spreaders and mast chocks.
2   Set the luff tension and cunningham so that small creases are just visible, and the draft is approximately 45% aft.
3   Stretch the foot out to within an inch or so of the black band.
4   Use the traveller to centre the boom on or slightly below the centreline, so that there is a small amount of weather helm.
5   Trim the mainsheet so that the outer end of the top batten is parallel with the end of the boom. Stitching coloured trim stripe over the pocket makes it more visible.

Jib

1   Tighten the forestay for optimum pointing.
2   Set the luff tension so the creases are just

removed (for flat water), and the draft is approximately 45% aft.
3   Set up the fore-and-aft sheeting so that the tell-tales all lift together.

CHANGING GEAR

You should always think of medium winds as maximum power conditions. Keep asking yourself throughout the race 'Can we handle more power now?' It is vital to have this question in your mind the whole time.

In keelboats it is easy for the helmsman to become locked into sailing the boat through the water, then look up and see that the boats to leeward have suddenly taken out a couple of lengths. In variable conditions one of the crew should be responsible for monitoring the rig constantly, and immediately the boat hits a lull the sails can be powered up to accommodate the change in windspeed.

The most obvious effects of a lull are:
•   The mainsail leech appears completely closed, and the top batten may be pointing a few degrees above the centreline.
•   The genoa leech, previously trimmed two inches off the spreaders, is just touching and the leech appears closed.
•   The genoa foot is creased up around the shrouds at deck level.
•   The boat is heeled less.
The crew's instant reaction should be to ease sheets a little to put the twist back into both sails.

Changes for light air

To power up the rig:
1   Straighten the mast to add depth to mainsail. In a dinghy add chocks in front of the mast. In a keelboat ease the runner or backstay tension.
2   Open the mainsail leech so the top telltale flies most of the time (Ease mainsheet and/or vang).
3   Pull the traveller to weather, to position the boom on the centreline for maximum pointing ability.
4   Add depth to the lower third of the mainsail. (Ease the clew outhaul two inches).
5   Add depth to the jib. (Move the lead forward and ease the sheet to keep the leech tension constant and twist off the upper leech.)
6   Move the jib lead to the maximum inboard position to improve pointing.

Heavy airs   Medium airs   Light airs

	Heavy airs	Medium airs	Light airs
Strut	up	down	up
Vang	hard	just tensioned	off
Cunningham	on	off	off
Mainsheet	just off	hard in	off (boom on quarter)
Outhaul	on	on	eased slightly
Jibsheet	ease	tight	ease
Barber-hauler	up	down	halfway

Changes for heavy air

The time to depower the rig is generally more evident than the need to make light air adjustments. In a blow the crew struggle to keep the boat flat and the boat moves sideways with each gust. The mainsail looks deep, the draft is too far aft and there is too much weather helm. To depower the rig:

1   Increase mast bend. (On a dinghy remove chocks in front of the mast and use the vang to promote bend low down. On a keelboat tighten the runners and/or backstay, and tighten the vang.

2   Pull the draft forward for more drive through the waves (pull on the cunningham).

3   Open the top of the leech to depower the sail and reduce weather helm. (On a dinghy pull on the cunningham. On a keelboat pull on the backstay and cunningham.)

4   Flatten the base of the mainsail (pull the clew outhaul out to the black band).

5   Reduce forestay sag. (On a dinghy increase rig tension. On a keelboat increase runner tension.)

6   Ease the diamonds (if fitted) to allow the topmast to fall off to leeward and open up the leech of the main. (This is effective on Contenders and Dragons).

5 Spinnakers

Unlike a fore-and-aft sail a spinnaker is often stalled over most of its area while it is flying. Even when close reaching, attached flow is present over only 60% of the sail. However, in some respects the spinnaker does behave like a genoa in that the draft can be pulled forward with luff tension, and the leech can be twisted open by raising the clew.

On the run

For running downwind, the spinnaker should be as big as possible, and set so as to achieve the maximum projected area to the wind. On a dead run the apparent wind is in the same direction as the true wind and the air is almost completely stalled in the sail. Because of this it is always faster to sail a few degrees closer to the wind and develop some airflow across the sail. To maximise the projected area flatten off the sail and pull back the pole (and ease out the sheet) to set as much of the spinnaker as possible out of the main's windshadow.

Reaching

The size and shape of the spinnaker is much more important on the reach. The deeper the middle of the sail the more power it produces, but at the expense of area. Pole height and angle are the two most critical controls when flying the spinnaker on the reach.

The sail should be full in the head to provide enough lift, so that it sets as far away from the rig as possible and does not backwind the main.

Choice of spinnaker

One-design spinnakers should be built to maximum luff and foot lengths but not necessarily to maximum mid-girth width. The amount of leeway allowed in the spinnaker mid-girth

(S.M.G.) will depend on the class rules, but it is commonly around 100 mm.

Small, narrow spinnakers can often be faster on close reaches. The reason is that with maxi spinnakers the slot between the spinnaker leech and mainsail is small; this means the main has to be overtrimmed to avoid backwinding, which cuts boat speed.

On an Olympic course, a small spinnaker which is easier to trim can give more speed on both the reach and run than a bigger kite which is more critical to trim.

When running downwind, a portion of the spinnaker is always hidden behind the main. In light airs this area does not fill and contributes zero lift. The sail is dragged down and prevented from filling properly. In heavy air the smaller kite is more stable to trim, there is less sail in the lee of the main, and the tendency to oscillate from side to side (known as the death roll), is reduced.

However, when broad reaching or running in medium air, the maximum-size spinnaker will generally be faster. Your choice of spinnaker will be a compromise based on the following factors:
- The type of course sailed.
- The number of spinnakers which can be carried under the class rules.
- The crew weight.

Matching the spinnaker to the race course

The Fireball and 470 classes illustrate the factors to be considered when matching spinnaker size to the type of course. Traditionally, Fireballs use a close-reaching course with a 60 degree gybe rather than the 90 degree gybe found on an Olympic course. As a result, small spinnakers have tended to predominate.

In the 470 class the question of size is a little more subjective. For the old Olympic course of two triangles, the majority of spinnakers were cut to the minimum S.M.G. with a few halfway

Above: A tri-radial spinnaker. The seams radiate from the head and clews.

Above: A cross-cut spinnaker. The seams are at right angles to the leeches.

between minimum and maximum. However, with the change in the Olympic course to only one triangle and a longer beat it seems in practice that the committee often fail to lay the gybe mark far enough from marks 1 and 3. The result is that the reaches become broader than 90 degrees. If this is the case, the fastest spinnaker is a sail laid out to halfway between minimum and maximum S.M.G.

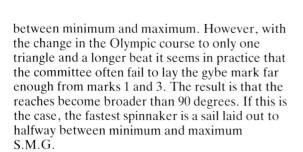

The author in action in the Rolex Commodores' Cup.

Tri-radials

While the majority of dinghies use cross-cut spinnakers, most keelboats use the tri-radial construction for reaching spinnakers because the extra loading caused by the heavy displacement would cause a cross-cut sail to distort dramatically. The purpose of the radial panel layout is the same as that of a radial-cut genoa. By aligning the strong thread lines in the cloth with the load lines in the sail, and by reducing the number of horizontal seams, cloth and seam stretch are reduced considerably. Cloth stretch can be further reduced by use of highly resinated or stabilised fabrics such as Dynac. This choice of cloth and construction produces a sail which will maintain, as far as possible, its designed shape under the high loads encountered on a close reach. If you use only one spinnaker on your particular class of keelboat, and you are principally interested in club racing around the cans, then the tri-radial will provide the best all-round performance and the longest competitive lifespan.

Cross-cuts

A cross-cut spinnaker is often preferred as a running sail. Large shoulders can be built onto a cross-cut and this is not so easy on a tri-radial. On the run the strength of the tri-radial is no longer required as the sail's loading decreases with the apparent windspeed. Because cloth and seam stretch are less of a problem, softer and sometimes lighter Nylon can be used. As the softer Nylon includes less resin, its actual weight is less than the more stabilised cloths. This allows the sail to set more readily in light airs.

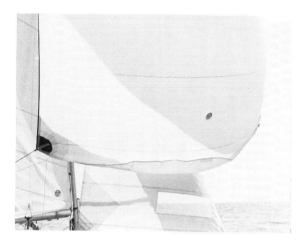

Above: A spherical cut spinnaker. The seams are at right angles to the centreline although there is no centre seam.

Dinghy cross-cuts

The reasons why dinghy spinnakers are generally cross-cut are:
- The reduced loads experienced by a dinghy sail do not warrant the tri-radial construction.
- It is possible to build shoulders on to the sail.
- In some cases, cloth stretch can be used to good effect.
- Cross-cut spinnakers are simpler and less expensive to build and develop.

There are two forms of cross-cut spinnaker. The true cross-cut has the panels arranged at right-angles to the leeches, and has a centre seam or 'mitre' down the middle. On the water the head panels appear to be cut in a chevron pattern. The alternative form of horizontal-panelled spinnaker is called the spherical-cut. This has no centre seam and the panels are aligned at right-angles to the centre fold instead of the leeches.

The major difference between the two is that the leeches will open much more on the spherical sail, as the cloth in the leech is orientated along the stretchy bias direction. The leech of the true cross-cut is orientated parallel to the stronger fill fibres, which are capable of withstanding higher loading.

There have been some very successful spherical-cut Flying Dutchman spinnakers, built from a soft and stretchy nylon. Cut to be relatively deep and full, the sail provides good power and lift on the broad reach and run. On heading up on a tight reach, the loads increase considerably on the sail, resulting in the luff stretching out flat and the leech twisting open more. Thus the sail is able to change shape automatically to suit the reaching and running legs.

Radial head

The radial head spinnaker is, if you like, a hybrid between a tri-radial and a spherical-cut. The radial panels in the head reduce stretch and control shape in the top of the sail, while the bottom is allowed to stretch a little more to create a deeper shape. This type of construction is little used these days, but has specialised applications

Above: A radial-head spinnaker.

on small keelboats, for example the mini spinnaker used on the Soling; it is also often used for Dragon running spinnakers.

Crew weight

Everything else being equal, a heavy crew can carry a larger spinnaker than lightweights. But it's seldom that everything else *is* equal, and spinnaker size is better determined by the skill of the crew.

Above: Tie the sheet close to the spinnaker clew, so the sail can be pulled right up to the pole.

Spinnaker fittings

On a dinghy you should use 5mm Kevlar for the spinnaker sheets, with a soft 8mm or 10mm tail for easy handling. The sheets should be tied directly to the sail to save the weight of clips or shackles, and to keep the distance between the pole-end and the corner of the sail to a minimum. If the boat has a chute you will require a retrieval patch in the centre of the sail, at least ten inches (25cm) in diameter. If the spinnaker sock is particularly short or the sail relatively large, it may pay to fit two puller patches. The lower patch should have a small cringle through which the retrieval line passes, up to the second patch, where it is tied onto a webbing loop. When the sail is doused, it is first retracted to less than half its original length, and it is then much quicker to pull it down into the sock.

On keelboats with more than one spinnaker, some form of clip or snap-shackle is unavoidable. 'Sister' or 'union' clips are used by many sailors;

they are fine until they become a little worn, when there is a danger that they may shake loose. Snap-shackles are a safer choice, especially for higher load applications, but be sure to choose a light but sufficiently strong model of minimum overall length.

In the Soling and Dragon the spinnaker can be launched from the cockpit, rolled into a tight bundle and secured by a Velcro tab. The package is thrown clear of the rig and hoisted halfway before a sharp tug on the guy causes the parcel to explode and the kite to set instantly. The system ensures that the sail is set fast and well away from the rig, minimising the chances of the spinnaker becoming ripped or twisted during the hoist.

When using both reaching and running kites on an Olympic course there is normally no need to repack a sail as the reacher is used for the first triangle only. The running sail is then ready for launching on the downward leg. Occasionally a major windshift on the first lap may necessitate using the runner first, so keep a laundry basket or launching bag on board in case you need to repack and launch the sail again.

With more than one spinnaker in the boat it is as well to have each one clearly marked on the corners to avoid clipping on the wrong sail when you are in a hurry.

Above: On a boat like the Soling, where more than one spinnaker is carried, use small, light, strong plastic snapshackles.

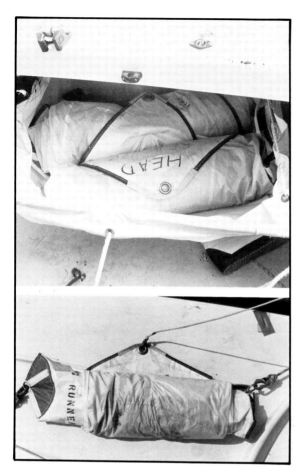

FLYING THE SPINNAKER (REACHING)

On the reach, set the pole height so that the spinnaker curls first halfway up the luff. If the sail breaks first below this point move the pole down; if above, move the pole up. The two clews should be approximately level, with the pole set horizontally on the mast if possible. Keep watching for the wind to shift aft and then move the pole back as soon as possible. The sheet should be played continuously so that the luff is always on the curl. Get into a rhythm of slowly easing the sheet out until the luff just breaks and then pulling it in. The sheet should never stop moving.

The time to pump the sail is when you feel a good surfing wave roll under the stern. The bow will dip and that is the moment for a sharp pump on the sheet to lift the bow up onto the wave. Remember, under ISAF rule 42.3(b) you are allowed no more than one pump per wave, and only when planing conditions exist.

Close reaching

The main aim when close reaching is to keep the slot between the spinnaker leech and mainsail as wide and as open as possible. If the slot is too small, the main will have to be overtrimmed, stalling the sail dramatically. In order to keep the slot open, try to keep the sail as far away from the boat as possible:

- Set the pole horizontally and low. If class rules permit, fit an extra eye on the mast above the standard one, or an adjustable track system. Tensioning the luff will encourage the clew to rise and twist the leech open.

Above: A Soling spinnaker is rolled into a bundle, secured with a Velcro tab, and stored in a launching bag.
Below: At the launch the spinnaker is lifted out of the bag, thrown outboard and hoisted halfway before the guy is struck to open the parcel.

Above: The pole is too high – the luff curls first below the half height.

Above: The pole is too low – the luft curls first above the half height.

- In medium conditions, let the spinnaker halyard off to move the head of the sail away from the mast.
- Make sure the sheet twinning line is off so the leech twists off and the clew moves outboard. The main boom then becomes the limiting factor on

Below: Close reaching in brisk conditions.

Below: On a light air run lower the pole to reduce the amount of unsupported area.

Above: When the pole height is correct the luff breaks evenly as the sheet is eased.

clew height, so ease the vang until the top batten becomes almost too open.

When using the small spinnaker in heavy airs many Soling crews allow the spinnaker sheet to ride up over the boom; this allows the leech to twist off sufficiently to keep the boat upright.

Running

When running in light airs there is insufficient wind to lift the spinnaker to its normal flying position, so the pole should be lowered to reduce the amount of unsupported area. The sail will then set more readily and provide a much greater projected area. As soon as there is enough breeze to lift the spinnaker, the pole should be moved up so that the clews are level and the pole horizontal. As before, the prime objective is to provide the maximum projected area, so bring the pole aft as soon as the wind has moved astern.

To keep the outboard end of the pole steady, the guy should be held down firmly near the shrouds by a hook or twinning line. Pulling the twinning line down after the gybe effectively pulls the guy further aft, so be sure to compensate by easing the guy before cleating it.

In heavy air the leeward twinning line is sometimes pulled on to prevent the sail from oscillating. In any case pull it on to make the sail more controllable when gybing. In strong winds the pole should be lifted to help the air escape from the top of the sail. If all the boats around you are broaching, try over-squaring the pole a little to flatten off the foot. But beware of over-doing it; if the chute collapses in heavy air it will start to flog and can take a long time to fill again.

Below: Running under spinnaker. (Left) the pole is too high. (Centre) the pole is too low. (Right) the pole is the right height for running in medium airs.

6 Fault finder

It is essential to recognise when a sail is not working correctly. Having isolated a fault, it is often possible to make changes in the rig adjustment to achieve correct trim. If the sail still does not look right it may need to be returned to the sailmaker for alteration.

MAINSAIL FAULTS

Luff curve does not fit mast bend

The most common fault sailmakers have to deal with is a luff curve which does not match the mast bend. Spotting the lack (or over-abundance) of luff curve is basically a matter of getting your eye in.

If the sail has too much luff curve the cloth will be tightly wrinkled just behind the mast because there is too much there. The mast needs to be pulled forward at this point to take the wrinkles away. This is achieved by pre-bending the mast a little more. An easy way on boats without adjustable spreaders is to move the heel of the mast back slightly, while keeping it fully chocked at deck level.

In the case of luff curve starvation the sail comes out very tight, like a board, from the back of the mast. There is just not enough cloth there, and there will be a crease running from clew to luff at this point.

The first step in curing this is to try to reduce the amount of pre-bend. However, this may not

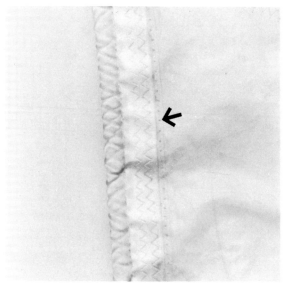

Left: Insufficient luff curve in this sail is causing wrinkles.
Above: This luff has been 'let out' to get more curve, leaving a telltale line of holes (arrowed).

always be desirable. Furthermore the luff curve may only require altering over a small area in order to match a particular mast's characteristics. In eight out of ten cases of sails not matching the mast, it is because the sail was originally designed around a different mast section.

Before getting the sail altered, take careful note of exactly how far up the mast the creases occur, or better still, take photographs in order to help the sailmaker judge how much alteration is required.

Finn sailors should be experts at spotting a fair luff curve, as it is a vital ingredient of a fast Finn sail. Finn masts are also notoriously individual, and the sail often has to be cut differently for each particular mast.

Loose leech

If the mainsail leech flutters upwind, try increasing the mainsheet tension or taking up some leechline (if fitted). When the mainsheet is hard on and the leech is still too loose (a common complaint with old sails which have stretched) the sail will flutter in between the battens.

Below: Mainsail leeches: loose (left) and tight (right).

To cure the problem note where the worst flutter occurs and then ask the sailmaker to put a few take-ups in the leech seams. This involves undoing the seam for about eight inches (20 cm) from the leech, moving the panels a few millimetres closer together and then reseaming.

If the leech now looks fine in light airs but continues to flutter in a breeze, the problem can often lie within the cloth. Perhaps surprisingly, one reason the leech does not stand firm is insufficient bias stretch – in other words the cloth is too firm in the 45 degree direction. This lack of stretch creates a flat leech which hinges open too soon. The only solution is to have a new sail made out of a cloth with greater bias stretch, this will produce a more rounded leech with a tight trailing edge.

Tight leech

Too tight a leech is a less common problem, but sometimes occurs in boats like 470s, where using normal mainsheet tension causes insufficient twist at the top batten. The cure is simply the reverse of a leech take-up: a let-out of a few millimetres at the offending seam.

Batten poke

Long creases running up the sail along the inboard ends of the battens are generally caused by too much batten poke. The sail has been cut with too much roach; this creates a sizeable compressive load, forcing the batten inwards into the sail. You can prove this is the cause if, when you pull the leech aft a few inches, the creases disappear.

Excessive batten poke usually occurs at the bottom batten, where the leech loads are greatest. It is for this reason that sails carry very little roach in that area. If your sail has too much roach it is a simple matter for your sailmaker to reduce it (although you do lose sail area).

Minor creasing at the batten ends can sometimes be solved by replacing bulky batten end fittings with tape.

Creases

No sail looks good with large creases running across it. A common complaint is 'over-bend creases' which run from the clew to just below the spreaders. These are caused by the mast bending too much in the lower section, pulling luff curve out of the sail and causing a line of tension from the clew. The solution is to either straighten the lower mast with extra chocks, or add more luff curve to the front of the sail.

Small creases originating from the clew patch but only carrying a few inches into the sail are due to cloth stretch in this high-load area. Better engineering of the reinforcement patch should prevent such creases.

Draft in wrong position

Draft position can be easily shifted from the 35% to 50% position through manipulation of luff tension. However, if your sail has the draft located at 20% aft when the luff tension is off, you have a problem! The sail will have very poor pointing ability, and in the case of a mainsail will show excessive backwinding. Unfortunately the cure involves major surgery to each broadseam, to move the point of maximum camber further aft.

Below: Jib leeches: a hooked leech (left) and a fluttering leech (right).

You can measure the exact draft position for yourself by photographing the sail from below. Lie in the bottom of the boat, and use a camera with a wide-angle lens, angled diagonally in order to get as much of the leech and luff in as possible. Check that the sail is sheeted correctly and is not luffing when you take the shot.

When you get the prints back draw the chord line in carefully, joining up the two ends of the trim stripe from leech to luff. (You can use the seams as trim stripes if none are present). With the chord line drawn in, move the ruler down the photo, holding it at right angles to the chord line (by sliding it along a set square) to find the position of maximum depth. Once you have found this point on the curve, join it with a line at right angles to the chord. This point now gives you the draft position and you can calculate the percentage draft position as shown in chapter 1. Similarly the depth can be measured and is also converted to a percentage of the total chord length.

Armed with this information, the sailmaker can evaluate the sail quickly and precisely, and he can

Below: Adding extra leech hollow.

decide if it is worth trying to recut it or not. Possibilities include altering the broadseam and changing the luff curve.

A feature of old sails is that the draft moves aft as the cloth breaks down and the bias stretch increases. For a while extra cunningham tension will help pull the draft forward to the original position.

JIB FAULTS

Hooked leach

If the jib leech has a significant hook to windward in light air this will increase drag and backwinding. (Any hook will blow out if the wind is strong enough). If the sail includes a leechline, the first step is to ensure that it is fully freed off. If the sail still hooks it is generally a sign of too much tension in the leech, often caused by the leech tape being too tight or the tape shrinking.

If the jib is new, it is worth asking the sail loft to fit a new leech tape and/or reduce the amount of leech hollow. However, the factors affecting jib leech curl are very critical, and it is not always an easy problem to solve.

As always the amount of leech tension placed in the sail through leech hollow is a compromise between too much, which causes the leech to hook, and too little, causing the leech to flutter. The firmer the cloth, the easier it is to produce a nice straight leech.

Old sails often develop a hooked leech as a result of cloth breakdown. To increase the life of the sail, the sailmaker can cut away the worn area by adding more leech hollow.

Jib leech flutter

Genoa or jib leeches will invariably flutter and vibrate at some point as the wind increases, due to cloth stretch. If your sail doesn't have a leech line and it begins to flutter very early in the wind range, the answer is to have some more hollow cut into the leech. This is a simple job, and in conjunction with a few leech take-ups can successfully rejuvenate an old and tired jib and curtail the fluttering.

Entry too fine

In the interests of improved performance to windward, headsails are being cut with finer and finer entries in an effort to improve pointing ability. These sails are what US sailors call 'fine groove': the margin between the sail luffing and the leeward side stalling is very small. Fine groove sails are great if you are a top helmsman sailing in flat water, but they often prove difficult to use in the majority of conditions.

Pulling the draft forward with luff tension will ease the problem, but will do little to change the actual luff angle of the sail. The best solution is to reduce the luff hollow by getting the sailmaker to put more cloth into the front of the genoa.

Conversely, if the front of the sail appears very full and the competition regularly points higher, you need to have more hollow cut into the luff.

SPINNAKER FAULTS

Shoulders fall in and collapse

To make the sail as large as possible, cross-cut spinnakers are cut with big 'shoulders' in the top. Shoulders are similar to the roach on a mainsail and need to be supported if the sail is to stand up in all conditions. To support large shoulders, the sail has to be cut quite flat in the top and this often results in creases radiating downwards from the head.

If the sail is designed to have large shoulders some creasing is inevitable, but if the shoulders are built too big without sufficient support from the body of the sail, the luff of the spinnaker will tend to collapse or, worse, it may not fly at all.

If your sail does collapse too quickly and feels very 'twitchy' to trim, have a look at the sail from off the boat and decide if the shoulders are too big. Look for the tell-tale creases from the head; these indicate that the shoulders are so big that they are pushing inwards, into the sail.

If the shoulders are too big, ask the sailmaker to re-fair the luffs. Alternatively a short take-up will round up the last few inches of the leech and increase stability.

Sail too full

A very deep spinnaker may appear to fly well, but seems to suffer from a general lack of performance, especially when running.

Below: The foot panel on this spinnaker is fluttering on a tight reach.

Below: The spinnaker tapes are too tight, causing the luff to hook.

A spinnaker which is too full in the middle and head will not project as great an area as a flatter sail. The luff and leech will appear rounded and tight, and the shoulders will appear very small. The deeper the spinnaker, the harder it is for the stalled airflow to move off the sail. A pocket of stagnant air may develop in the deepest part of the sail and as a result, any flow across the sail is reduced.

The performance of a sail which is marginally too full can be improved by over-squaring the pole a little. The further apart you trim the leech and luff, the flatter the sail will fly. A spinnaker which is much too full will have to be completely re-cut, and all the broadseams will have to be reduced.

Hooked luff or leech

If the luff of the spinnaker appears hooked or curled the chances are that the luff tapes are too tight. The reason could be that the thread tension is too tight or poor-quality tapes have been used which shrink on wetting.

To rectify the problem the luff tapes have to be removed and resewn very carefully with a loose but even tension.

Foot panel flutters on close reach

Another common complaint with spinnakers is that the foot panel flaps noisily as the boat heads up onto a close reach. What happens is that the foot is stretched out tight, forming a crease between the two clews. Any cloth below that line which is unsupported and held in less tension will flap in the breeze.

To cure the problem, ask your sailmaker to increase the tension throughout the foot panel and put some shape into it by taking in a couple of vertical darts. Alternatively, the amount of unsupported foot round could be reduced, although this means losing some projected area when running downwind.

Below: This spinnaker is backwinding the main excessively. The barber hauler should be let off and the pole lowered to encourage the clew to fly up and to leeward.

7 Yacht genoas

The most important factor to consider when you are buying headsails for your cruiser/racer is the rule you will be racing under: is it a one-design class, IRC, IMS (or the new IRM rule), PHRF or a local club handicap? You need to know because certain handicap systems and classes penalise laminated sailcloths, or prohibit 'hi-tech' aramide fibres such as Kevlar and Spectra in the interests of limiting expense.

The International Measurement System (IMS), and some restrictive classes such as the ILC 40ft class, can be considered 'type forming rules':

they tend to produce boats with broadly similar lines and sailplans. So any modern IMS boat designed to race competitively will always carry a 150 per cent overlap Kevlar genoa as there is no rating advantage in using a smaller Dacron sail in the same conditions. In fact, the only reason we are so used to seeing 150 per cent genoas on all sorts of boats these days is because that is the size the IOR originally said a headsail should be. Upwind, a 100 per cent jib actually makes for a more efficient sailplan than the overlapping 150 per cent genoa. Many recent production cruiser/racers, built without any regard for the IOR, are using 100 per cent blade jibs on self-tacking tracks, often with large-roached, fully battened mainsails. Specific cruiser/racer rating systems such as IRC, PHRF and IMS all allow so-called exotic sails, but under IRC the boat may carry a rating penalty for each carbon fibre sail on board. The way the rule is worded is also important. The IRC system asks the question 'Do any sails contain hi-tech sailcloth?', whereas the IMS does not differentiate between woven and non-woven fabrics but does penalise sails which it considers to be lighter than the norm. The weight rule is likely to be dropped under the new IRM rule.

Is a laminate genoa worth carrying?

The first point to consider is the size of your boat. Boats under 28 feet are usually better off with an all-purpose Dacron No.1 genoa, for the following reasons:·

● For the loads on this size of rig there is no significant weight-saving advantage to Mylar. Typically you could either use 3.8oz Mylar or 4.4oz yarn-tempered Dacron.

● As only one No.1 is carried on a 28-footer, it has to be an all-purpose sail, capable of having its shape changed for use across a whole range of conditions. A Kevlar sail is often so stable that its shape cannot be altered much.

● As crew weight is a higher proportion of the boat's total displacement on a small yacht, the No.1 genoa is carried higher up the wind range than on a larger yacht. In other words, with all the crew sitting out, a 28-foot boat can hang on to the same No.1 to around 22 knots.

● A laminate headsail designed for a specific wind range will always be slightly faster than an all-purpose Dacron sail, but it may not provide enough extra pace to offset the speed

lost through changing and carrying multiple genoas for various wind ranges.

Above the 30-foot mark, the advantages of more stable, less stretchy and lighter headsails are sufficient to offset any increase in cost for a laminated genoa fabric. Mylar seems preferable to Kevlar or Spectra on this size of sail; a pure Mylar sail is quite capable of withstanding the loads generated (assuming the correct weight of Mylar has been used) so the higher cost for Kevlar is not worth considering. However, when it comes to the No.3 jib, the expense of aramide fibres is worth it, for a corresponding Dacron No.3 would be significantly heavier and would not hold its shape like a Kevlar sail.

Of course, every handicap rule is different so

it is worth looking closely at a selection of your local fleet's measurement certificates before deciding on the exact balance between performance, rating and budget. The IMS rule, for instance, does not penalise exotic sails at all but it does include a sail weight factor which is incorporated in the Velocity Prediction Program (VPP) input. If an IMS sail is much lighter than the chosen norm, this has an effect on the overall handicap. For this reason an ideal IMS sail might be a light-bodied Kevlar sail with heavy luff tapes and big, overbuilt hardware at the corners to bring the weight up to match that of a Dacron sail.

In the USA the most popular cruiser/racer handicap rule is the PHRF system, with over 15,000 boats rated. It is an empirical rule based upon actual observations of how each yacht performs in its regional area. The basic idea is that a light-air flyer will be more heavily handicapped when sailing in a typical 8-knot breeze in Chesapeake Bay but have a smaller rating when competing in 25 knots in San Francisco. PHRF does not penalise non-woven sailcloth at all, and most of the fleet can be seen sporting Mylar and Kevlar sails. The US rule begins to penalise genoas when they reach 160 per cent or bigger, and as a result most PHRF No.1's have a 155 per cent overlap.

Fabric choice

The layout of a genoa is dictated by the chosen fabric. There is a continually evolving range of Mylar, Kevlar and now Spectra laminates available, alone and in many combinations, all designed for different applications. Some are straight warp-orientated, uni-directional fabrics laminated onto Polyester/Dacron or Mylar substrates. Others use a zig-zag Kevlar thread which spreads the warp load across 12 degrees.

However, before getting too carried away with exotic materials, give some thought to the conditions and wind range you need the sail to perform best in. Do not choose a stiff, stable front-end material if you really want an all-purpose genoa. In light airs and a lumpy sea it may be impossible to introduce extra depth and drive into the luff of such a sail. But don't panic! Such tricky decisions are what you pay the sail designer for. He will advise you, but get him to explain the reasons for his fabric selection to you. An understanding of how the material of your new headsail works will help you get the best performance out of it.

Shape

Every sail designer has his own ideas on the latest fast shapes, although the trendiest designs are often amazingly similar to those being used five years previously. Using computer-aided design systems sailmakers can easily reproduce fast, proven genoa shapes. If the sail loft is part of an international group it should be possible to reproduce say, the light No. 1 design that won the 50-foot class in the US last year, for your new genoa being built in Australia.

For the typical cruiser/racer owner, it is important to ensure that the headsail shape you are given suits:
- The conditions the boat usually sails in.
- The style and abilities of the helmsman.
- The shape and weight of the hull.

Below: A fine entry on the genoa (left) gives better pointing, but a full entry (below) is more forgiving and a better choice unless you are really confident of your helmsmanship.

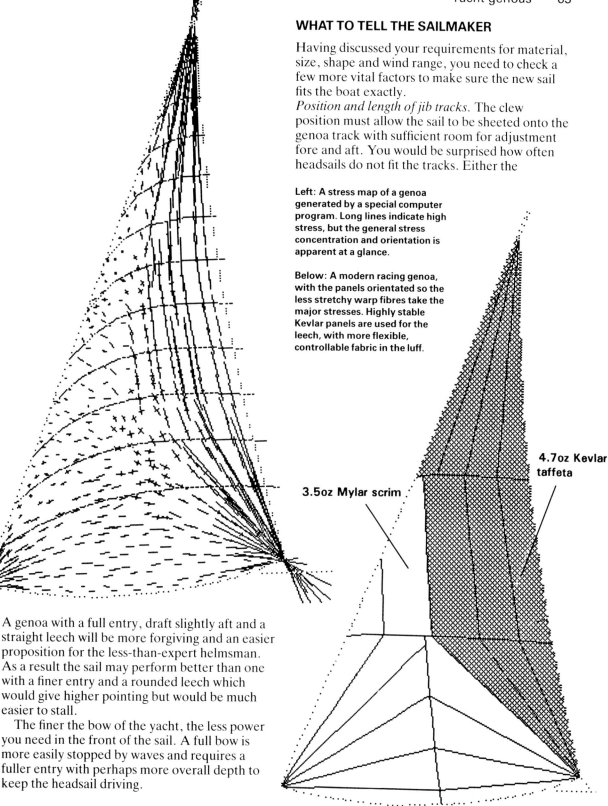

WHAT TO TELL THE SAILMAKER

Having discussed your requirements for material, size, shape and wind range, you need to check a few more vital factors to make sure the new sail fits the boat exactly.

Position and length of jib tracks. The clew position must allow the sail to be sheeted onto the genoa track with sufficient room for adjustment fore and aft. You would be surprised how often headsails do not fit the tracks. Either the

Left: A stress map of a genoa generated by a special computer program. Long lines indicate high stress, but the general stress concentration and orientation is apparent at a glance.

Below: A modern racing genoa, with the panels orientated so the less stretchy warp fibres take the major stresses. Highly stable Kevlar panels are used for the leech, with more flexible, controllable fabric in the luff.

4.7oz Kevlar taffeta

3.5oz Mylar scrim

A genoa with a full entry, draft slightly aft and a straight leech will be more forgiving and an easier proposition for the less-than-expert helmsman. As a result the sail may perform better than one with a finer entry and a rounded leech which would give higher pointing but would be much easier to stall.

The finer the bow of the yacht, the less power you need in the front of the sail. A full bow is more easily stopped by waves and requires a fuller entry with perhaps more overall depth to keep the headsail driving.

sailmaker gets it wrong, using a sailplan which does not correspond exactly to the boat, or the owner orders a 150 per cent genoa for a production boat which only comes with tracks for a 100 per cent jib! If in doubt, measure from the tack fitting to both the front and rear of the track. If there is no sail plan, you need to measure the position of the track from the centreline, relative to that of the shroud base. This is so the sail designer can put enough shape in the bottom of the sail for it to sheet around the shrouds, rather than up tight against them.

Amount of mast rake. It is critical to know the 'pin to pin' dimension of the forestay to ensure that the clew ends up in the right place: nice and low to the deck, but with enough room to sheet it properly. As the mast is raked back, the genoa clew drops. Make sure the sailmaker gets the message; he may assume that because the last boat of this class that he made sails for was sailing around with a lot of rake, this one will be too!

Forestay sag and running backstays. The sail designer needs to know the amount of sag the boat sails with, so that the luff curve can be cut to match. This can be measured from photographs of the boat upwind, from head on. The designer will also need to know whether running backstays are fitted.

The number, height and position of the spreaders. This information should be on the sail plan, but it is amazing how many rig versions are built of the same production boat. Likewise IOR boats often change spreader lengths and number. These measurements allow the sail designer to build in enough twist so that the leech does not foul the top spreader, and enough leech hollow so that the sail sheets just inside the middle or bottom spreader.

Type of headfoil or luff system. This is so the correct-sized luff tape is fitted. If furling gear is used, the genoa luff length will have to be cut shorter to accommodate the drum at the tack and the swivel at the head. Incidentally, it is as well to check that there is always some luff tape hanging below the feed-in to the headfoil. If the bottom of the luff tape disappears inside the foil, it can be almost impossible to get the sail down!

Hardware requirements. Do you need a snap hook or a shackle at the tack? Does the clew ring have to take a snap shackle?

Below: Measure from the tack fitting to the normal genoa car position, plus the front and rear of the track, and give the measurements to the sailmaker.

Below: Ensure there is some luff tape protruding from the headfoil groove when the sail is fully hoisted. If not, the sail may jam when you try to get it down.

Above: When you hoist the genoa make sure the bowman helps the luff tape into the pre-feeder to prevent damage to the sail. Hoist the sail quickly from the mast, using the winch to apply the final tension to the halyard.

Spreader end and stanchion position. With laminated sails it is important that spreader patches are fitted in the right places before the sail is used. I have seen many a genoa holed first time up, because the enthusiastic new owner did not take the time to fit the sticky patches supplied. *Sail number.* Most handicap rules require sail numbers on headsails bigger than 100 per cent overlap.

SHEETING THE GENOA

The simplest starting point for setting any headsail is to position the fairlead so that an extension of the sheet would intersect the luff in the middle. The mid point is often marked by the second trim stripe down from the head, so use this as a sight guide. Stand back and, using a sail batten as a straight edge, sight along the line of the genoa sheet and see where the line would cut the luff. Some sailmakers even draw the correct angle onto the clew patch to make things easier.

Right: With the genoa sheet fairlead in its starting position an extension of the sheet would intersect the luff halfway up.

Once you have found this initial setting, you can fine-tune the lead position by slowly luffing the boat and checking that the tell-tales all lift together, as we saw in Chapter 4. (In fact the top tell-tale should lift a fraction before the bottom, as the head of the genoa carries more twist than the bottom.)

The principles of sail trim are the same whatever boat you sail, but cruiser/racers have their own particular set of problems.

As the majority of popular dual-purpose yachts are one-designs or production boats, the genoa tracks are seldom in the best position for good sail trim. Other factors such as the size of the accommodation tend to take precedence. Most one-design class rules do not allow you to move the tracks, and most production yachts are limited to a single track on each side, commonly at an angle to the centreline of more than the optimal 8–9 degrees. So in flat water and 8 knots, how do you sheet the genoa to point higher? Here it pays to take an imaginative approach.

First decide where you would ideally like to sheet the genoa. Measure the angle of the track to the boat's centreline and then see how much further it needs to come inboard to get to 8 degrees. Now you are probably somewhere between the track and the coachroof grab rail. Somehow, you must find a way to sheet the sail to this position. What you need is a snatch block with a short sheet, which you can use to rig a temporary barber-hauler to bring the lead inboard in optimum pointing conditions. When

Below: Here a snatch block lashed to the coachroof grab rail is used to barber-haul the genoa sheet inboard to improve pointing in 8–10 knots of breeze and flat water. The effect is to pull the clew in and match the genoa twist to that of the main (right).

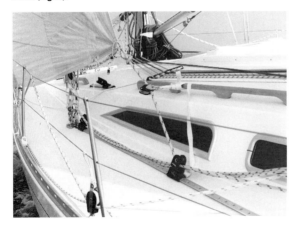

led back to a spare winch, this simple arrangement allows an almost infinite variety of lead positions.

Sheeting the genoa closer to the centreline can give your boat an immediate and significant advantage over other boats in the fleet. However, do not hold on to it for too long if the breeze increases. As soon as the front of the mainsail starts to lift noticeably (which is an indication that the lee side pressure is getting too great), it is time to go back to sheeting directly to the track.

On a two-sail reach, you can use the same snatch block to sheet the eased genoa as far outboard as possible. Clip the block onto the toerail, forward of the upwind car position. This arrangement will always be a compromise since the ideal lead position is about three feet outside the boat, but it is worth making every effort to get as close as possible to this ideal. Otherwise you will give away an easy advantage to the opposition.

Below: On a two-sail reach use the spinnaker guy to sheet the genoa as far outboard as possible. Lead it well forward through a snatch block on the toe rail to increase leech tension and control the twist in the upper leech. Here (right) the genoa twist matches the main nicely.

Below: a combination of genoa sheet and spinnaker guy tension gives you a wide range of adjustment. Watch the telltales: if the top one is always flying first the top of the sail is too open and you need more leech tension; if it flies last you need less leech tension.

The photos on these pages show the correct lead position for various wind conditions on a Sigma 38.

1 Starting position. The angle of the sheet meets the luff at the mid point. Medium wind speed setting, 12–18 knots.

2 Move the lead aft one hole for more wind, 19–20 knots plus. On this one-design boat the genoa car can only be moved by hand, between the factory holes provided. With such coarse adjustment, one hole forward or aft of the standard position is all you generally use. Avoid the tendency to strap the sheet in more as the wind builds by easing the sheet to twist the leech open. Monitor the angle of heel and speed of the boats around you. If they are sailing flatter and faster, the chances are they are sailing with more twist.

3 Sheet forward, to power up the middle of the genoa in light and/or lumpy conditions. If you are sailing a one-design with the same track and hole positions as the rest of the fleet keep an eye out at the start to see how the fast boats are set up.

If conditions change during the race and one boat suddenly becomes faster or slower, look to see where his genoa car is. With experience you will get to know the exact wind strength for each car position, but do not forget the wave state. A short chop will require more power from the headsail than flat water.

Below: Moving the car aft in heavier airs eases the leech and tightens the foot. This puts more twist into the top of the sail and flattens the base. Note the position of the leech compared to the lower spreader.

Below: In 12–15 knots and flat water move the genoa car forward to create a tight, rounded leech and power up the middle of the sail. Note how far in the sail is compared to the end of the lower spreader.

4 Barber-haul the lead inboard in optimum pointing conditions (see page 66). In this case 8–10 knots apparent and flat water. Never come in further than 8 degrees and make sure you know how far that is on your boat. On the Sigma 38 in the photo, the clew should not come inside the genoa track.

5 Barber-haul to the toerail for two-sail reaching (see page 67). Limit the excessive leech twist by moving the snatch block for the lead well forward.

Once the genoa has been set up with the optimum amount of twist by correct positioning of the genoa car, the other headsail controls come into play.

Sheet tension

Sheet tension is the dynamic control over sail shape: it should be adjusted in response to every change in windspeed and direction. The photo opposite shows what a well-trimmed genoa should look like in an apparent wind speed of 12 knots. The leech is firm but not too closed, set 2–3 inches off the spreader; the middle is quite deep and powered up, just touching the shroud base. The amount of twist matches the twist in the main.

The quickest way to respond to a drop in windspeed is to ease the sheet so that the leech remains in the same position, 4–5 inches off the spreader. As the leech load is reduced, easing the sheet will rapidly restore the original amount of twist to the sail.

Halyard tension

We have already seen, in Chapter 4, how halyard tension is used to set the draft position in the sail, moving it aft to around 47 per cent for high pointing or forward to 40–43 per cent for a powerful shape.

If you are used to sailing with Dacron headsails and then move up to Mylar or Kevlar, you will find the range of halyard adjustment much reduced. To move the draft on a Dacron genoa from a light to heavy airs setting entails moving the halyard at least 6–8 inches, but a Mylar sail needs only 2–3 inches of adjustment to keep the draft constant as the breeze increases. This is because Mylar does not stretch as much as Dacron and does not allow the draft to move aft so quickly as the loading builds. In the case of a very low-stretch Kevlar or Spectra sail, adjusting the halyard may have little obvious effect.

Match-mark the headfoil and luff tape so you can set the sail with the same tension at each hoist or use it as a reference mark for changes in luff tension.

If your yacht carries running backstays these can be used to fine-tune the halyard tension. Although the runners primarily control forestay sag and in turn the angle of entry to the genoa, they also affect the sail's depth. Straightening the forestay pulls the luff further away from the leech, so flattening the sail.

It is worth remembering that there are several occasions, other than heavy air or lumpy seas, when it is fast to set the draft forward in the

Below: Increasing halyard tension pulls the draft forward in the sail; here it is 15% at 44% aft.

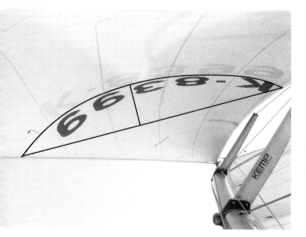

Below: With the halyard eased the draft moves back – in this case to 52% aft.

Above: With the runners completely eased the mast straightens up and the forestay slackens. The resulting luff sag puts more shape in the front of the genoa, making it more powerful when pointing is not the priority.

genoa. When two-sail reaching you should ease the runners to get the genoa as full and powerful as possible.

THE GENOA TRIMMER

A good genoa trimmer is a sailor with a keen eye for sail shape, strong powers of concentration and the experience to know how his sail should be set up in every condition. He is responsible for the whole inventory of headsails, from making sure they are properly flaked ready for swift changes, to ensuring they set to perfection. He should oversee all sail changes and alterations to lead positions, and he should get to know each sail's wind range and advise the skipper in good time when a change may be necessary.

If you are the trimmer, sailing with a new helmsman, discuss with him how he wishes you to trim for particular conditions. For instance, if the boat is sailing across a long wave pattern, he may want you to ease the sheet a few inches as the bow goes over the back of each wave and then wind it in as the boat heads up the front of the next one. Such techniques need to be carefully co-ordinated with the helmsman to ensure you are both working together. Similarly, in a shifty breeze it can be faster if the trimmer responds to each lift by easing the sheet to maintain a constant twist, rather than waiting for the helm to luff up. Talk to the helmsman as you trim so he knows what you are doing; this will ensure that you are not working against each other.

The more advanced the racing, the faster the boat, the better the helmsman and the more instruments available, the harder the trimmer's job becomes. Not only does he have to monitor boatspeed to ensure the trim is correct, but he has to decide where the balance should lie between speed and pointing. A read-out of VMG (Velocity Made Good) can be useful but an easier and more immediate measure of relative performance is to watch the speed and pointing of those boats around you. When trimming, I like to have one of the crew on the rail regularly update me on the speed and angle of a known boat nearby. This information tells me when to move from speed to pointing mode as the tactics dictate.

Finally the trimmer should always remember that his weight is an important part of the boat's righting moment. The lighter the yacht, the more important it is that all the crew are up on the windward side. At around 18 knots, the genoa

Above: Good cockpit communication is vital. The helmsman, mainsheet and genoa trimmer must liaise with each other all the time – and the genoa trimmer has to respond to each shift or gust before the helmsman.

Above: Cross winching – take the genoa sheet around the windward winch to allow the trimmer to keep his weight to windward while playing the genoa. This is especially important on a breezy two-sail reach.

trimmer has a critical choice to make between sitting to leeward and trimming or cleating the sail and climbing up to the windward rail. If the windspeed is steady, set the genoa up after the tack, wait for the boat to regain hull speed, check again that all looks good, then cleat it and move swiftly to the high side. Every time you feel the genoa needs a tweak, you need to decide whether the transfer of your weight to leeward and the correction to the trim will result in a net increase in speed. If not, then stay where you are.

One answer to this dilemma is to cross winch to the windward side but this can make tacking messy. Another answer is to fit a spreader window in the main, so that the trimmer can keep an eye on the genoa leech from the rail and then dive to leeward to adjust the trim only when necessary. Even better would be to have a windward sheeting fine-tune system which uses a block and tackle to move the genoa turning block, but such arrangements are rare on production offshore yachts.

Special conditions: wind shear

The worst problem the genoa trimmer has to deal with is excessive wind shear. Very occasionally weather conditions will create considerable wind shear near the surface when warm air off the land is suddenly cooled over the water and becomes very stable. This can make it almost impossible to set the genoa, as I discovered while crewing a one-tonner on one occasion. The clew had to be held up on the centreline, with so much twist that the top of the sail was on a reach. On the other tack the effect was reversed and I had to try and sheet the sail so that the upper leech was hard in and the bottom of the sail was 20 degrees further off the wind. Luckily such large variations in wind angle and speed with height are rare, but it is important to realise when shear is playing a part. If you find that the genoa needs to be twisted more on one tack than the other, shear is probably the culprit.

Light airs

Most cruiser/racers have the shroud base set aft of the mast to support the mast more safely. This means that with the rig tension wound up it is hard to encourage the forestay to sag off in light airs to put extra fullness into the front of the genoa. So, the trick in a drifter is to take a spare halyard onto the bow and winch it up as tight as possible, pulling the mast forward and slackening the forestay. This will allow the luff to sag to leeward, powering up the front of the sail.

8 Yacht mainsails

When it comes to the choice and trimming of the mainsail on a big boat, much the same considerations apply as with a genoa: the sail is big and expensive, so you need to make the most of your investment by choosing wisely and learning how to get the best out of your final choice.

BUYING THE RIGHT MAINSAIL

Many cruiser/racers in the 28–38 foot range which carry laminated headsails still use Dacron mainsails, for although the benefits of less stretch and reduced weight aloft that 'plastic' provides are well worth having, such factors are not always the most important. Much more important is the type of rig and the weight and shape of the hull.

A low-stretch, laminated mainsail is a very different beast to sail with than a conventional Dacron main. Instead of using the sail controls to trim the main for different windspeeds, you have to bend the mast to adjust the sail's designed shape. So to get the best out of a Kevlar or Mylar sail your boat must be equipped with a flexible and easily adjustable spar.

Dual-purpose yachts tend to be more heavily rigged than racing boats, with stiffer, less tweaky spars whose shape cannot be altered dramatically on the water. Such rigs are therefore more suitable for Dacron mains which can have their shape changed using the sail controls. Racing boats, with their more flexible masts, are much better suited to Kevlar or Mylar, for it is easier to set up the mast around the main.

If your boat is a cruiser/racer, then, you are probably better off with a Dacron main. But if it is a racer/cruiser, rather than the other way around, with a relatively flexible mast, then your choice of mainsail fabric is more open. It is now possible under the Channel Handicap rule to make multiple applications for rating certificates, so that you can check the exact effect of either a laminate or Dacron sail on the rating.

When choosing a racing mainsail for a yacht over 40 feet long, however, the benefits of Kevlar generally outweigh those of Dacron. The biggest difference is that the Kevlar sail will hold its designed shape much better than the Dacron version. The working loads experienced on a 40-foot plus rig will begin to distort a Dacron sail in even the lightest breeze. In 25 knots the sail shape will be so severely overloaded that it becomes impossible to set the sail correctly. Weight also becomes a significant factor: a Kevlar cruiser/racer mainsail will weigh around 28–30kg for a 44-footer, while a cross-cut Dacron equivalent will be around 20 per cent heavier.

Dacron mainsails – radial or cross-cut?

In recent years several sail lofts have been building radial-cut Dacron mainsails, with the aim of limiting stretch by using warp-orientated panels with the number of seams crossing load lines reduced to one or two. However, after several years of experience with such designs some sailmakers are finding that radial mainsails in purely woven, vertical Dacron do not hold their shape as long as was once envisaged.

The reason for this is that mainsail Dacron does in fact stretch quite significantly in the warp direction. This is because it is hard to keep tension in the very long warp threads as they are stretched out the full length of the factory while the fill threads are inter-woven. This does not apply to the firmer genoa styles or coated finishes, where more resin is used to limit bias stretch.

This is not to say that all radial Dacron mainsails have this problem. Improved fabrics come onto the market every year, one example being the warp-insertion fabrics which employ large-diameter warp threads laminated on top of the standard weave to inhibit warp stretch. Square weave resin coated Dacron (in which the stretch is equal in the warp and fill) is often the best cloth for radial mains, as the high resin

content permits little movement. Resin coated
Dacron also lasts longer in a mainsail than in a
genoa; in a main it does not flog so much and does
not get dragged around the rig at each tack.

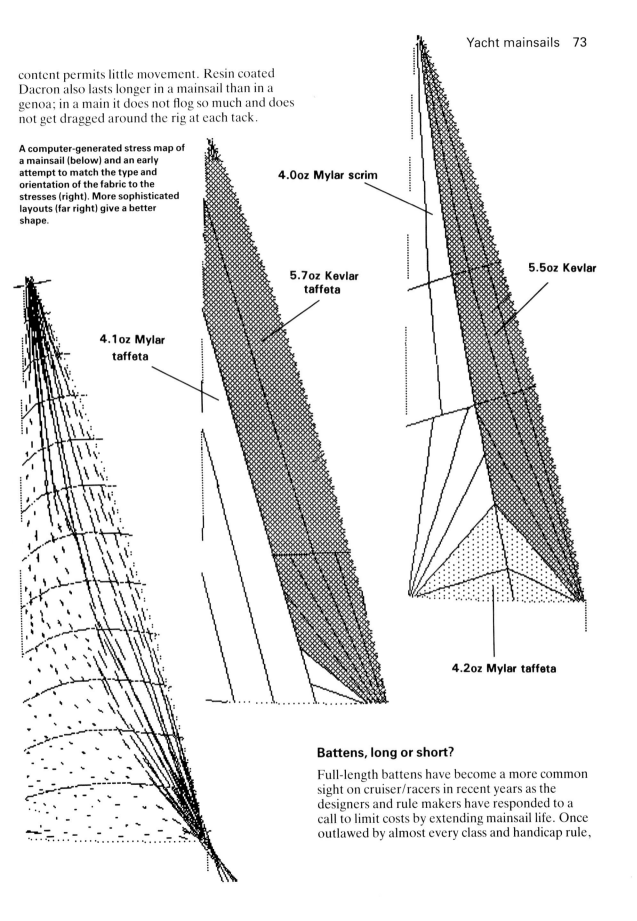

A computer-generated stress map of
a mainsail (below) and an early
attempt to match the type and
orientation of the fabric to the
stresses (right). More sophisticated
layouts (far right) give a better
shape.

4.0oz Mylar scrim

5.5oz Kevlar

**5.7oz Kevlar
taffeta**

**4.1oz Mylar
taffeta**

4.2oz Mylar taffeta

Battens, long or short?

Full-length battens have become a more common
sight on cruiser/racers in recent years as the
designers and rule makers have responded to a
call to limit costs by extending mainsail life. Once
outlawed by almost every class and handicap rule,

full-length battens are now allowed by PHRF, IMS and numerous production one-design classes without penalty.

In the early days of fully-battened mainsails the technology of connecting the batten ends to the mast was dismally inadequate, causing all sorts of problems. Robin Knox-Johnstone remembers roaring up the Thames Estuary in his 60-foot cat *British Airways*, only to find that the huge fully-battened main refused to come down because the loading on the batten end slides caused them to

jam solid. Now every hardware company produces its own custom batten fittings and cars which ease the problem considerably.

The benefits of full-length battens are:
1   Reduced flogging of the sail, giving a longer life.
2   Sail shape in heavy air is improved because the designed shape is locked in.
3   Ease of handling when reefing, dropping and flaking the sail, especially when short-handed.

However, serious racing sailors have found that they need a variety of batten stiffnesses for different windspeeds: battens stiff enough to support the leech upwind often appear too stiff offwind, preventing the mainsail leech from twisting open. As the technology of tapered carbon and Kevlar battens develops, the idea that long battens save you money begins to look a bit thin. Full-length battens on production boats also have cost-related problems, in that the manufacturers often use low-specification batten and car hardware to keep the list price down. This can result in the battens distorting the sail and restricting the effect of the normal sail controls.

The final choice of battens will depend on the particular boat and the rule under which the mainsail will be measure. Large-roached mainsails, such as those used on the America's Cup class yachts, obviously require long battens to support the compression from the leech. But if the rules prohibit wide-girthed mainsails then there is little point in choosing full-length battens for a fully-crewed racing boat. The longer batten lengths introduced a few years back, and now adopted by most rating systems, do a good job of improving both the shape and life of the mainsail.

TRIMMING THE MAIN

The photographs on these pages show the correct way to set up the main for a variety of upwind conditions.
1   Light airs trim (8 knots apparent, flat water). Set the outhaul tight, about one inch from maximum. Twist the main well open by pulling the traveller to windward and easing the mainsheet and vang. The boom should be on the centreline and the luff tension should be slack. Slacken the runners and tie them forward out of the way, but tension the permanent backstay 25 per cent to bend the top of the mast and help

open the top of the leech. In very light airs it is vital that the leech is kept open and does not hook up owing to the weight of the boom hanging down. The best way of combating this problem is a solid gas strut vang which can lift the boom; alternatively rig a spare halyard to the end of the boom. I have even won a race using a broom propped underneath the boom end!

2   Medium airs trim (18 knots apparent, flat water). Power up the main and reduce twist: the end of the top batten should be in line with the boom, with the outhaul on hard to flatten the middle and lower leech, the traveller eased but the boom still on the centreline, the vang on fairly hard to control leech tension, the runners firm to tighten the forestay and bend the mast a little, the luff loose, the backstay off to close the top leech and the mainsheet played to maintain a constant twist.

3   Medium airs and waves (18 knots apparent). In these conditions the yacht needs more power at the expense of pointing ability. So compared with medium-airs trim, the mainsail needs:

● More twist, with the mainsheet and vang eased so that the top batten is open and the telltale flies all the time.

● Greater depth in the middle and top sections, which you create by easing the runners and also, if necessary, the outhaul.

● The traveller a little further down the track to reduce weather helm; this will help the helmsman sail lower and reduce heel for extra drive.

● The halyard tightened to move the draft forward for a more powerful shape.

4   Heavy airs (25 knots apparent plus, with waves). The photograph shows the main nicely bladed out and flattened off, with an acceptable amount of lifting at the luff; the traveller is well down the track to ease the helm and keep the boat as level as possible. In this case the leech is being bladed out (flattened and twisted off, but with the edge of the leech still driving) by heavy vang tension, a technique known as vang

Below: Trimmed for 8 knots of breeze, with the traveller up, the sheet eased to give lots of twist, the vang fairly slack, runners off to give a straight mast, and some of the crew weight to leeward to maintain the heel.

Below: Medium airs – 18 knots or so – and flat water. The mainsheet is pulled on to tighten up the leech and bring the top batten parallel with the boom end, the traveller is halfway down the track to create an even slot with the genoa, the runners are on but fairly soft, and there is some vang tension.

Below: The set-up for heavy airs, with the vang and runners fully on, the main 'bladed' out (i.e. flat and well twisted) with the front third just lifting, and the traveller fully to leeward.

Above: The leech is too tight for the windstrength – the top batten is hooked to windward and there is not enough twist.

Above: The mainsail set about right for the conditions, with the correct amount of twist. The top telltale is just flying and the top batten is parallel with the boom.

Above: Here the mainsail leech is far too loose, seriously impairing the boat's pointing ability.

sheeting. With the leech tension set purely by the vang, the mainsheet is left to control boom angle. On this boat, using the mainsheet coarse tune in this way provides a much quicker response to gusts than playing the traveller. However, the vang *must* be released before bearing off, or you can lose the rig!

The other sail controls are set as follows. The luff tension tight with the cunningham on to pull the draft back to where it should be and to open the top leech; the outhaul out to the black band; the runners on as hard as you dare; and the backstay on enough to help open the leech, but not so much that the last inch of the sail begins to flap. Although the rest of the sail can be inverted in a gust it is imperative that you keep this part of the leech driving, for without it all pointing is lost and the yacht will slip rapidly sideways.

The mainsheet trimmer

I always enjoy doing mainsheet on a racing yacht. You get a snug seat at the back of the boat, shielded from the spray by the rest of the crew, you are next to the helmsman and tactician and it is up to you alone to set the main properly. Unfortunately if you get it wrong it is only too obvious, especially with a Kevlar main which is either set or not. Serious lack of speed, pointing, or big creases in the sail are immediately noticed by the team on the rail – who then become experts and offer all sorts of conflicting advice!

Left: Trimming the main, using the traveller (right hand) and mainsheet fine tune (left hand).

The answer is to work closely with the helmsman. You will quickly earn his confidence if you keep asking him how the helm feels and if he wants speed or pointing. If he replies that the helm is heavy (too much weather helm), try easing the traveller down or flattening the base of the main by tightening the outhaul. Liaise with the headsail trimmer at all times. You must also work with the tactician, who may ask for speed or pointing to hold clear air or lay a mark.

The two set-ups for speed and pointing have already been discussed, but it may help to recap. To move from speed to pointing mode do the following:

1   Squeeze the runners harder and ease the backstay to firm up the leech.
2   Ease the luff tension so the draft is at 50 per cent.
3   Position the boom nearer to the centreline if the windstrength and heel angle allow.
4   Close up the top leech a little by trimming the mainsheet and/or tightening the vang.

Below: Here the runners have been wound on too hard for the windstrength, resulting in an overbent mast, the classic luff curve starvation creases and a main that is far too flat for the wind conditions (12 knots). With the runners completely eased (right) the mast is straight, the sail depth is right and the rig is fully powered up.

Above: Winding the clew outhaul tight (left) flattens the base of the sail and opens the lower leech. Easing it a few inches (right) serves to round up the lower leech, giving more feel on the helm for steering in light airs. The base of the sail is also deeper.

In the absence of any tactical reasons for one mode rather than the other, it is up to the mainsheet trimmer to maintain a good speed *and* angle. The setting of the main is always a compromise between speed and height, so you need to keep your eyes fixed on the sail to check the amount of twist. Ask one of the crew on the rail to monitor the speed and pointing of rival boats; this will allow you to watch the sail constantly while receiving a constant measure of the boat's performance. If your skipper decides to be the only boat to go the other way, however, you will have no other yachts to check your performance against and you will have to resort to instruments or the polar diagram.

Polar diagrams

A polar diagram is simply a graphic plot which shows the speed at which the boat should be going for each windspeed and wind angle. You can build up your own set of polar curves by noting the best speed you achieve for each condition and then updating your figures whenever you surpass the previous recorded speed. Alternatively, any yacht that applies for an IMS certificate can obtain a free, individually prepared polar diagram. Otherwise the boat's designer may have a design programme that can automatically generate polar curves.

Sailing on instruments or 'polars' will be a more common experience for handicap racers who have few comparable boats to sail against, or during offshore races when the fleet spreads out of view. But the best indication of performance will always be the other boats in the race, if you are close enough to them.

Above: Instruments and polars are very useful, but your best boatspeed indicators are your rivals in the fleet.

TACKING THE MAIN

In light to medium breezes it is important to ease a couple of feet of sheet as you go into the tack, to provide more power into and out of the turn. Once the boat has tacked, the trimmer's first act should be to pull the traveller up to the original setting. This provides the vital feel on the helm so the helmsman can come back up onto the wind. If the trimmer is slow with the traveller, the boat can lose ground to windward by sailing too low out of the tack.

In heavy conditions it may not be necessary to ease sheet through the tack, as the yacht is already overpowered. Similarly, there is no need to bring the traveller back up in a hurry; it will only create more heel and leeway. Wait until the crew are all up on the weather rail and the boat is better balanced.

Above: Before the tack the cockpit crew sets up the new winches and gets ready to tail the new genoa sheet.

The trimmer eases the mainsheet two feet or so to power up the main into the tack.

The mainsheet trimmer moves across as the helmsman tacks the boat.

Above: In full sail, with the main and No. 1 – this case a 135% genoa.

Above: Full main and No. 2 (100% blade jib)For sailing in waves the No. 2 is sheeted between the shrouds onto the front of the No. 1 track to open the slot and allow more twist.

ORDER OF REEFING

A well-organised crew should have a proven sequence for reducing sail, based on a memorised set of windspeeds for each sail change. Obviously the actual sequence depends on each individual yacht, sail and wave state but for a Sigma 38 cruiser/racer the order is something like this:

- 0–24 knots apparent:· Full main and 135% A.P. No.1.
- 22–26 knots apparent: Full main and 100% No.2 blade jib, sheeted onto the coach roof jib track (in flat water).

The trimmer brings the traveller up to the correct position . . .

. . . Then adjusts the mainsheet fine tune for the new tack once the boat is up to speed.

Finally he checks the twist, since it may need a different setting on the new tack owing to wind shear.

Above: One reef in the main and the No. 2 (100% blade jib), for sailing in 30–35 knots apparent wind.

Above: A heavy airs set-up, with reefed main and No. 3 (80% working jib).

- 26–30 knots apparent: Full main (bladed out), and 100% blade jib sheeted through the shrouds onto the front of the No.1 track (or earlier in waves).
- 30–35 knots apparent: One reef in main and 100% blade jib.
- 35 knots apparent plus: One reef in main and 80% working jib.

DOWNWARD TRIM

When it comes to the offwind legs, the vang takes over from the mainsheet as the primary twist control. The further off the wind you are sailing, the more you ease the vang; when you are running you should just use it in heavy air to prevent the top of the main twisting in front of the mast, since this makes the boat roll. Keep the top batten at 90 degrees to the centreline.

Right: When sailing downwind it is important to get the rig as far forward as possible to raise the sail plan and reduce the effect of upwind rake – so shackle the genoa halyard to the tack fitting and winch it as tight as you dare.

Ease the other mainsail controls to power up the sail but do not let the clew in so far that the projected area is reduced. Let the mainsheet out until the front begins to lift and then play it from there. Too many mainsail trimmers leave the sheet cleated downwind, and lose speed as a result.

On a shy spinnaker reach the vang is the critical speed control. In medium winds it pays to slightly oversheet the main, so that it does not close the slot formed with the spinnaker leech. You can then control the power developed by the sail by standing up on the windward rail, next to the spinnaker trimmer, and playing the vang in tandem with the kite. In this position your weight is better placed to keep the boat flat, and you can see any approaching gusts in time to dump the vang and prevent the end of the boom hitting the water. You will also be better placed to avoid a broach.

Below: In light airs the weight of the boom can cause the mainsail leech to hook up badly when running, preventing the air from exhausting freely and causing the sail to stall (see right).

Below: Use a halyard (or a gas strut vang) to lift the boom end; this will allow the leech to open until the top batten is at 90 degrees to the centreline. But don't let the sail twist off in front of the mast or the yacht will roll.

TARGET BOATSPEED, VMG AND THE POLAR DIAGRAM

Once the crew has sorted out the rig and knows where and how to sheet the sails the next big jump in performance comes from ensuring that the boat is sailing at its optimum speed and angle all the time.

To do this you need some way of checking your target boatspeed for every wind angle and windspeed, and the simplest method is to use a polar diagram. The term 'polar' refers to the way the three scales are centred around the origin. Basically it tells you not only how fast your boat should be going, say upwind in 10 knots, but also the optimum angle to sail to reach the windward mark soonest. In other words, it provides a measure of velocity made good, or VMG.

Looking at example diagram, we can see that in

Below: A typical polar diagram, with curves for five wind speeds. The horizontal scale shows boatspeed, with the scale repeated on the lines marking 15-degree sectors. The arrows indicate the optimum downwind angle for each windspeed.

10 knots of true wind our yacht should be doing about 6.2 knots, at an angle of 44°. If we sail higher, the curve rapidly heads back towards the origin and the boatspeed slows. Bear off and the graph shows how the speed builds as the heading becomes broader.

The optimum angle to sail for the 10-knot windspeed (assuming average wave conditions) is the angle marked on the curve. This point is simply the highest part of the curve, up the vertical axis.

Target boatspeed

To simplify matters you could write a series of target boatspeeds, for upwind and downwind, on the bulkhead near the cockpit instruments. These figures should be taken from the polar diagram. They will help you a lot, since they will show up any problem – such as an oversheeted main – before the opposition starts to overhaul you.

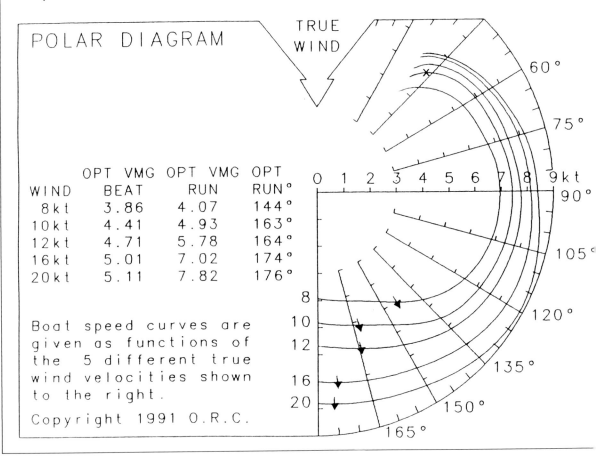

POLAR DIAGRAM

TRUE WIND

WIND	OPT VMG BEAT	OPT VMG RUN	OPT RUN°
8 kt	3.86	4.07	144°
10 kt	4.41	4.93	163°
12 kt	4.71	5.78	164°
16 kt	5.01	7.02	174°
20 kt	5.11	7.82	176°

Boat speed curves are given as functions of the 5 different true wind velocities shown to the right.

Copyright 1991 O.R.C.

wind speed	btn	boat speed	vmg
6	140	4.1	3.2
8	144	5.0	4.0
10	163	5.2	4.9
12	164	6.0	5.8
14	170	6.6	6.5
16	174	7.0	7.0
20	176	7.8	7.8

Above: A simple set of polars written on the bulkhead for quick reference from the helm.

The information to generate the polar diagram comes from a Velocity Prediction Program (VPP) which uses actual measurements taken from individual yachts. Since many of the dimensions required by the VPP are the same as those taken for an IMS rating, the RORC Rating Office in the UK or the USYRU in the USA can provide individual polar diagrams for any yacht with an IMS certificate. The other way to obtain a possibly more accurate polar diagram is to contact the boat's designer, who will have used similar computer software in the design process to predict the eventual performance.

The VPP naturally makes certain assumptions, such as wave height and sail efficiency. Hence it will be impossible to hit target boatspeed while sailing upwind in an awkward, left-over slop. Similarly, if your sails are old and distorted you may never be able to hit the targets in high windspeeds.

VMG (velocity made good)

Not long ago, a VMG instrument was the latest readout to have on the boat. However, its use can be at best confusing and at worst detrimental to performance.

If you are using polars and target boatspeeds there is no real need for a VMG instrument, since VMG can be easily read off the diagram. What's more, trying to steer off a VMG readout can be counter-productive as it teaches the helmsman to pinch upwind. As the yacht heads up the VMG improves as the two vectors become closer, but if the boat continues to head up the sails will luff and stall out, boatspeed drops and VMG crashes as a result (see diagram).

If you do have a VMG readout on the boat, the way to use it is to find the point at which VMG is just about to decrease: that will be the optimum VMG. But keep an eye on the boatspeed repeater at all times.

Using the information

As this is a book on sails and not on instruments, how can this information help us improve sail trim?

1   If you find it harder and harder to hit your boat's target speeds upwind, it may be an indication that your genoa is becoming old and stretched. (Assuming all other variables remain constant, e.g. hull condition and instrument calibration.)

2   Similarly, if the boat can no longer hit her target speeds downwind, then maybe it is time for a new kite. Too much rake on the mast can have a similar effect.

3   If you buy a new sail you can compare its performance to the last one – as long as you have a written record of the speeds you achieved with it. When you are assessing a number of headsails it can be a big help to accurately measure in which windspeeds each sail hits the target speed. This helps you make decisions regarding the range and performance of different genoa designs.

4   If your boat is sailing faster than the target speed it generally means that you are sailing too low upwind, so head up to maximise VMG (and vice versa downwind).

5   Lastly, if you are sailing the angle the polar diagram suggests and you are still faster than the target speed, pat yourself on the back and re-draw the curve! The yacht's target speeds should be updated every time the polar figures are bettered, when a sail is changed or when conditions are not typical.

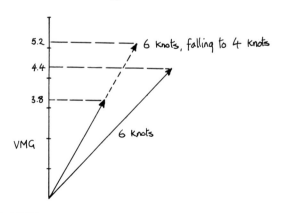

9 Yacht spinnakers

We looked at the principles of spinnaker trim for dinghies and keelboats in chapter five. Big-boat spinnakers are trimmed in exactly the same way, and a good dinghy or keelboat crew can swiftly make the transition to trimming a yacht's kite. The only differences to get used to are the size of the sail and the different gybing techniques.

Flying a big kite calls for good teamwork and co-ordination, as three crew are needed to help trim the spinnaker and up to six during a gybe.

CHOICE OF SPINNAKER

For the same historical reasons that the 150 per cent genoa has become the standard No.1 size (due to the trend-setting IOR rule), all the major handicap systems follow the IOR spinnaker formula, which dictates the shape of the spinnaker we all use. The dimensions of an IOR-type chute are:

Luff length (LL) = $\sqrt{(I^2 + J^2)} \times 0.95$
Spinnaker mid-width (SMW) = $1.8 \times J$

(I = Forestay length; J = Distance between base of forestay and front of mast.)

This method of measurement explains why masthead boats have tall, thin looking kites, due to the long luff length factor (I). The modern design trend towards shorter J dimensions also results in spinnakers with narrow girths. Several top designers argue that the IOR dimensions prohibit the development of more efficient spinnakers. You only have to look at one-design yachts such as the First Class Europe to see the performance advantage of a wider girth.

The IRC rule penalises spinnakers with girths exceeding the old IOR maximum. There is also an extra penalty if more than three kites are carried on board while racing. Almost every handicap system penalises poles which are longer than the J dimension, and many one-design cruiser/racers with long class poles require a second, J length pole for handicap racing.

A typical cruiser/racer downwind inventory of two sails would be:
1   0.9oz all-purpose spinnaker, 0–18 knots apparent.
2   1.5oz all-purpose spinnaker, 16–30 knots apparent.
Keen racer/cruiser boats, such as custom IMS yachts, are more likely to have a three-sail inventory:
1   0.5oz all-purpose spinnaker, 0–12 knots apparent.
2   0.9oz all-purpose spinnaker, 8–18 knots apparent.
3   1.5oz all-purpose spinnaker, perhaps with a narrower head angle for close reaching and heavy air running, 18–30 knots apparent.

With a maximum of three sails allowed under most cruiser/racer handicap rules, there is no room for specialised reaching or running sails, so all the spinnakers have to be equally at home on a reach or run (i.e. all-purpose). Such an inventory merely provides a range of cloth weights to cover the range of wind strengths. However, with such a variation in apparent windspeeds downwind (owing to the wide range of true wind angles) each spinnaker can be used for specific conditions.

For example, sailing in a true wind of 12 knots the apparent windspeed on a 90-degree reach could be around 17 knots. You would therefore have the 0.9oz kite up, and be thinking about the 1.5oz if the breeze came up any more. If the next leg was a dead run the boatspeed would drop to around 5 knots and as a result the apparent wind speed would also go down to around 7 knots. So to get the best speed out of the boat, if say you were struggling against a foul tide and chop, you should peel to the 0.5oz kite which will be easier to fly and more responsive to trim.

The decision as to which kite to hoist is based on the apparent windspeed and angle of each leg. Tactical considerations should also be considered. In a close one-design fleet on a short Olympic course, you may lose more during the change than you gain from using the lighter sail. Polar diagrams are of great value downwind, especially when stepping onto a new or unfamiliar yacht where you are unsure of the optimum running angles or target boat-speeds. They can tell you the optimum angle to steer on the run for a given wind speed; as you can see from the diagram the basic rule is that you can sail lower as the breeze becomes stronger.

These days it is impossible to list a standard spinnaker inventory for an IMS race boat as the choice will depend entirely upon the form of the racing. An inventory for the Admiral's Cup is limited to four sails in total, which could be:

1   0.5oz all-purpose.
2   0.75oz reacher/runner.
3   1.5oz Mylar reacher.
4   0.9oz heavy runner.

Mylar spinnakers became popular in the 1980s in IOR racing but are now seldom seem. Being stronger and less stretchy than nylon the response time from trimming the sheet to the sail moving is reduced. As a result the boat is faster. However, as with all Mylar sails the stable fabric means that the spinnaker tends to have one fixed, specialised shape. The lack of 'give' in the fabric also means that a Mylar kite may be more likely to split when overloaded by a gust. So although a Mylar spinnaker should be faster than its nylon counterpart in any given wind strength, it remains too specialised a sail for a cruiser/racer.

Construction

Almost every yacht spinnaker built these days uses some form of tri-radial construction. Cross-cut kites can cope with the loads on small, light displacement boats, such as J 24s and Etchells, but above that size the loads involved demand the cloth to be cut on the warp.

In the same way that a genoa panel orientation is matched to the load map of the sail, so too is the spinnaker's layout. The loads are clearly concentrated in the head and clew areas and are handled perfectly by the radial panels and patches. Where the loads spread out and become reduced in the middle of the sail it is possible to

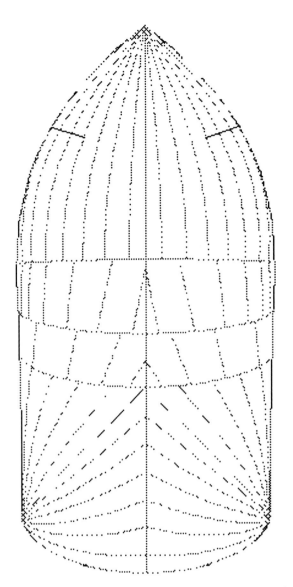

Above: A modern tri-radial spinnaker plan, with two rows of 'rocked' centre panels and leech take-ups at the top quarter-height.

horizontal panels around onto the warp. This saves a huge amount of time, as each 18-inch section has to be 'rocked' by a slightly different angle, from 90 degrees at the luff to 80 degrees at the centre seam, and this is laborious to do by hand.

Some sailmakers have developed entirely radial spinnakers with a single joining seam, but these have proved hard to match to the load lines in the sail. The current state of the art is a tri-radial sail with two or more changes of warp orientation through the cross panels depending on the size and aspect ratio of the kite. These are known as two-cut or three-cut sails.

It is increasingly common practice to cut a take-up into each luff of a spinnaker at the top quarter-height in order to round up the edge of the luff. This technique can give a previously twitchy, flat, broad-shouldered kite a more elliptical section, making it easier to trim. Adding a take-up means that less hollow is required in the luff, giving wider quarter section and three-quarter section girths. It is a good way around the problem that when a designer flattens the spinnaker, to give a greater projected area, it generally becomes critical to trim. A spinnaker which is easy to trim is likely to be in correct trim for a greater proportion of the time and for that reason alone it is often the fastest sail.

COMMON TRIM FAULTS

The correct way to fly the spinnaker for each wind angle has been discussed in Chapter 5. Novice yacht crews seem to have the same kite handling problems, which are always brought to light when the breeze gets up and the pressure is on.

Coping on the shy reach

How many times have you seen a crew desperately trying to hang onto a collapsed and flogging spinnaker on a close reach? The way to avoid the situation is to make sure you never get into it. As you approach the gybe mark before heading up to the reach you must prepare the boat and crew for the sudden increase in apparent windspeed and change in wind angle as follows:
1   Flatten off the main as for the beat. Position someone ready on the rail with the tail from the vang, ready to dump it if required.
2   Set up the spinnaker: drop the pole to tension the luff, tension the topping lift and downhaul so

use horizontal panels, but this does mean that the load is suddenly applied in the stretchy bias direction and this results in some distortion. The original reason for the horizontal panels in the middle of the sail was that they provided a convenient way of putting the shape in, and involved less work than an all-radial sail. With the coming of computer-aided design and automatic cutting it has become a lot easier to turn the

that the pole is locked and cannot sky, ease out six inches of halyard to let the sail fly further away from the boat, let the leeward twinning line right up, move the sheet to the biggest winch on the windward side and position the grinder as far to windward as possible.

3 Get all the crew onto the rail, with legs out, ready to harden up.

4 Slowly let the pole go forward to a point just off the forestay as the boat heads up.

5 The spinnaker trimmer can call to the helmsman to bear off in the gusts and head up in the lulls as he feels the pressure begin to build through the sheet.

6 As a gust hits, concentrate on hiking hard and keeping the boat flat and the yacht will rapidly

Above: Good close reaching technique, with (1) the pole low and just off the headstay; (2) the sheet led well aft to allow the clew to rise up and the leech to twist off; (3) the halyard eased four inches to get the kite as far away from the main as possible; (4) the trimmer well forward and outboard where he can see the sail and help the weight distribution; (5) the mainsheet trimmer standing up to play the vang – the quickest way of powering and depowering the main; (6) the rest of the crew hiking.

accelerate. If anyone leans inboard to ease the main or wind a leeward sheet winch, the boat will simply heel more, the keel will stall out and she could broach.

A windy beam reach is the most exhilarating point of sailing, once you are confident that the crew and not the wind is in control.

Above: Gybing – raise the inboard end of the pole to the marks to allow the outer end to swing under the forestay.

The bowman trips the guy and pulls the pole end towards him, using the genoa sheets hanging over the pole.

The bowman shouts "Made" as he clips the new guy into the pole end.

Dip pole gybing

The only way to perfect your gybes is to keep practising in all wind strengths, because the technique varies between light and heavy airs.

A common fault is for the winch and guy tailers to be looking down and not forward. This means that they are not co-ordinated with the action on the foredeck and either haul in too early, ripping the new guy out of the bowman's hands, or are too slow to ease the kite forward.

The answer is to delay the gybe until everyone is ready and knows their precise role. Practise slow, controlled gybes before trying to build up speed. Hold the main in the middle of the boat in light airs, so as not to collapse the kite through the gybe.

It is vital to set the pole immediately at the right height and angle as the boat comes out of the gybe and tension the downhaul so that the kite does not collapse or lose speed.

Below: The hoist – first raise the pole to the right height for the reach.

The bowman lifts the outboard end as the mastman tensions the topping lift from the cockpit.

Sneak the guy back behind the genoa as you approach the mark. Watch the kite does not blow away too soon.

Before the hoist the clew must be at the end of the pole, and the pole squared at the correct angle.

The pole is pulled round by the mastman and squared by hauling on the guy from the cockpit.

The mastman readjusts the pole height for the new gybe.

In light airs square the pole slowly to avoid shaking and possibly collapsing the kite.

Hoisting the spinnaker

As soon as the skipper is sure that he can make the windward mark you should prepare for the hoist. Raise the pole to the correct height for the expected reach; it is important that the pole is locked solid in this position by tensioning the topping lift and downhaul. A few lengths from the mark, the crewman on the guy should start to sneak it back, pulling the clew out from behind the genoa. If he times it correctly, the clew should be at the end of the pole as the hoist is called. It may be necessary to have one crewman to leeward holding onto the rest of the kite to stop it from blowing away from the boat too soon.

The crewman on the sheet must remember to ease out lots of sheet as the sail is hoisted, before trying to sheet in. Try to resist the tendency to pull the sheet in during the nervous apprehension of the few seconds before the call for the hoist.

Raise the halyard by hand, standing at the mast, with someone in the cockpit tailing the

Hoist the spinnaker quickly by hand at the mast while the cockpit crew tail the winch.

Once the sail is up, sheet in. Then drop the genoa as soon as possible to stop it interfering with the kite.

The spinnaker trimmer should move forward to a point where he can see the whole of the spinnaker luff, so he can trim the sail effectively.

And away you go!

Above: Make sure the pole is always horizontal to maximize the projected sail area.

Above: As soon as the pole is off the forestay start hauling the twinning line down on the sheet to bring the sheeting angle forward and create a more powerful running sail.

winch. It is vital that the guy is back as the kite goes up, for it will never fill quickly if it is hidden in the lee of the genoa. To help the kite fill do not ease the genoa too soon; holding the genoa in also helps the bow bear away around the mark without having to use a lot of rudder.

As the spinnaker goes up drop the genoa swiftly to avoid further disturbance, and immediately clip the genoa halyard onto the tack fitting. Tensioned as hard as possible, the halyard pulls the rig forward to alleviate the negative effect of the upwind rake. The rig should be pulled forward on every downwind angle other than when the pole is on the forestay.

Correct sheet lead position

When you are reaching with the pole 40 degrees off the forestay, start bringing the sheet lead forward by pulling down the twinning line. Just as with a genoa, moving the lead forward tightens the leech of the kite, eases the foot and allows the base of the sail to become fuller. Tension the leech in this way, and the luff via pole height, to add depth to the sail and provide more power. On the run the spinnaker should be made as powerful as possible in all but the heaviest winds. Select the pole height that keeps the luff breaking at the half height first. Closer to the wind you will need more twist in the leech to flatten and depower the sail, so lead the sheet to the stern.

If the boat is not fitted with twinning lines, use a snatch block to bring the sheet forward to a position on the toerail or simply switch over to sheeting on the lazy guy.

Preparation and packing

Always start the race with the sheets, guys and halyard clipped together on the guardrail on the appropriate side and the guy clipped into the pole. There is no need for the bowman to be scurrying around the foredeck halfway up the beat, when it can all be set up before the start. If it is necessary to change the gear over, it is already clipped together and can be pulled around from the windward side.

Likewise if you know which spinnaker you are likely to be using, hang it up just inside the hatch, so it can be quickly grabbed from on deck.

A useful aid to re-packing the kite is to screw three hooks in the cabin to hold the clews and head while you are chasing down the luffs. This makes the packing a quick one-man operation.

10 Care and repair

While modern sailcloth may appear very tough, it is a mistake to believe that sails do not need to be looked after. All sails, whether Dacron or Mylar, should be rinsed in fresh water after exposure to salt water or dirt. Any salt crystals left within the weave will chafe the adjacent fibres, causing premature cloth breakdown. The hygroscopic (water-attracting) salt crystals prevent the sails from drying off properly, causing corrosion of any metal fittings on the sail such as press rings (eyes) and headboard rivets.

FOLDING AND STORING

After washing and drying, yarn tempered sails should be carefully rolled from the head down. You can leave the battens in to help support the rolled sail and prevent it from being folded. As the resin dressing holds the fabric so stiffly, any tight creases tend to crack the finish and break the underlying fibres. Most creases occur while

Above: Mylar or yarn tempered sails should be rolled to prevent the formation of tight creases.

moving the sails around, so the best place to store them is inside a roll bag, laid out in the boat, under the cover. Mainsails made of softer cloth

Left and below: Soft sails made of a material such as Dacron should be loosely flaked concertina-style, then rolled into a loose bundle.

can be loosely flaked rather than rolled, as long as you use a different fold line each time. This method produces a lot of non-permanent creases which blow out easily.

Sailmakers will always tell you not to leave sails flogging on the boat, as this greatly accelerates cloth breakdown. Take your sails down while the boat is on the beach. Many sailors wrap their jibs around the forestay before launching or in between races. This practice is fine in light airs, but if you leave your jib furled on a windy day, you may come back after lunch to find the sail half unwound, flogging violently from side to side and the forestay chafing through the luff.

PREVENTING WEAR AND TEAR

To ensure that your brand new sails do not get ripped first time up, scour the boat for any sharp projections, and remove them or tape them up. The worst offenders are cotter pins, broken wire strands and projecting screw heads. Pay particular attention to the area around the spinnaker chute or bags, and make sure the spreader tips are well taped.

Spreader patches

You would be amazed at how may new sails come back to the sail loft for repair because the spreader has poked through the leech first time up, the owner having failed to fit the spreader patches supplied.

Spreader patches are only necessary on boats with large overlapping genoas, which can get pinned against the spreader when the sail is backed for too long. Sailmakers normally supply the self-adhesive Dacron patches loose with the sail, as

Right: Teflon tape prevents the spinnaker pole chafing the jib luff.
Below: A flutter patch prevents the seam stretching at the leech, where the load is greatest.

the correct position will vary from boat to boat depending on spreader height and mast rake. One-design boats which often require spreader patches include International 14s, Dragons and J24s.

To fit a patch, hoist the sail, mark where the spreader tip touches the leech and note the angle at which the patch should be set. Next, take the sail down and find a clean, flat surface where you can smooth the sail out flat. Working from the inboard end, peel a few inches of the backing paper off the patch and stick the end down in the chosen position. Check the patch is angled correctly; if not, there is still time to rip it off and try again. Then slowly peel the backing paper off towards the leech, pushing any air bubbles out from under the cloth as you go. At the leech cut the cloth flush. Then repeat the process for the other side of the sail, wrapping the last inch of cloth around the leech.

It is especially important to protect laminate mainsails with spreader patches. Remember that offshore mainsails with two or three reef points will require extra spreader patches for each reef position. The most likely time for the sail to be damaged is if it flogs wildly as the reef is taken in.

Jib luff protection

A common area of chafe on many dinghies is on the jib luff tape, where the spinnaker pole rubs against the luff wire and cuts through the cloth. One answer is to use plastic-coated wire, but it is then impossible to use a tension meter on the forestay.

The best solution is to get your sailmaker to fit a section of Teflon tape over the affected area, which is tough enough to cope with any amount of chafe.

Care of luff tapes

The luff tape is the most easily damaged part of any headsail. Such damage is often caused by a hasty hoist by a careless crew, but it can be avoided by taking the following precautions:

- As the headsail is hoisted make sure there is enough slack jibsheet, and that the trimmer does not wind it in before the sail is fully up. Otherwise the luff tape can be ripped or pulled out of the headfoil.

- When tensioning the genoa halyard, do not wind it up so tight that the tail of the luff tape disappears up inside the headfoil. If this happens, you are guaranteed half an hour of wrestling with the headfoil to get the tape out before the sail can come down.

- It is often hard to adjust the luff tension in both main and genoa while beating in a medium or strong breeze. You can winch the halyard bar tight without getting the wrinkles out of the luff, owing to the friction inside the luff groove created by the sail's loading. The trick is to ask the helmsman to luff the boat briefly to reduce the load while you tension the halyard.

- Take great care not to wind up the main halyard so hard that the hard eye is pulled through the sheave, jamming or even breaking it. At the end of the day it is faster to put up with a few unwanted creases in the luff than have the mainsail fall down halfway up the beat.

- Take the same care with the outhaul; and always watch the corner of the sail as you are winding it out. I have witnessed numerous occasions when, with the adrenalin pumping, the grinder grunts the winch as hard as he can, only to be rewarded with a loud explosion as the outhaul/flattener/halyard suddenly fails.

Battens

It is a sailmaker's nightmare to see battens flying out of his mainsail as the sail flogs before the start. At important regattas you should take no chances and sew the battens in with a quick stitch, or tape across the pocket.

Changing sail numbers

Removing numbers from a sail is not as easy as one might imagine. The cloth will peel off fairly easily, but the adhesive layer is invariably left firmly stuck to the sail. The only way to remove this sticky mess is to soak the area in acetone or carbon tetracholoride until the glue becomes loosened and can be scraped off. Be careful to

Below: Applying sail numbers and letters. (1) Smooth the sail out on a flat surface, and carefully position the number. (2-4) Begin to peel off the backing paper (starting at the top). Stick the top edge of the number to the sail then gradually peel off the paper, allowing the number to 'fall' onto the sail. If the shape is complex, cut the backing paper so you apply one half at a time.

1

2

3

4

place a plastic sheet underneath the sail when using the solvent, as stains and marks from the floor can wash through into the sail. When the acetone has dried off, the new numbers can be applied. Check that the spacing between the numbers is in keeping with the class rules and that the number is located correctly on the sail. If there is no mention in the class rules, then the ISAF Appendix HI.3 applies: 'Class insignia, national letters and sail numbers shall when possible be wholly above an arc whose centre is the head point and whose radius is 60% of the leech length. They shall be placed at different heights on the two sides of the sail, those on the starboard side being uppermost..... National letters shall be placed above the sail number.'

Some regatta sailors like their sail numbers placed as close as possible to the leech, so that their numbers are not so easily taken if they are caught over on the start line!

RUNNING REPAIRS

Damaged and torn sails are best repaired by the sail loft which built them. If a whole panel needs to be replaced it can be re-cut accurately from the original pattern, and the cloth can be matched exactly.

However, according to Sod's Law, you are most likely to rip a sail half-way through a regatta, when you have come ashore at 6 pm, the next race is at 10 am the following morning, and the local sailmaker has already left for the cheese and wine reception! The answer is to carry your own sail repair kit and learn how to deal with minor repairs yourself.

Ask the sailmaker for some off-cuts of your mainsail, jib and spinnaker cloth, suitable for patching. You may be able to buy a ready-made repair kit, and if possible it should include:

- Patch cloth for main, jib and spinnaker
- Self-adhesive insignia cloth and tape
- Spinnaker repair tape
- Spinnaker luff tape
- Webbing
- Hand-sewing needle and thread
- Pins

Spare hardware:
- Clew slug
- Batten end protector
- Spare battens
- Extra telltales
- Silicon spray
- Double-sided sticky tape for seams
- Press rings or grommets and tools

Small holes or chafe patches can be held together temporarily with self-adhesive insignia cloth; larger rips have to be cut out and replaced by a 'window patch', for which you will need a sewing machine.

Applying a window patch

1. Take the damaged area and pin it out flat on a smooth surface. Decide on the size of the patch, which should be kept clear of seams if possible.

1

Left and below: Repairing a hole. (1) Laying out the damaged sail. (2) Preparing the patch. (3) Sticking the patch over the hole. (4) Cutting back the damaged material.

2

3

4

Ensure the direction of weave in the patch matches the sail (i.e. the warp and fill threads line up) and trim the patch to size.

2. Apply double-sided tape to the edges of the patch and stick it down flat. Unpin the sail and hold up the patched area to check there are no bumps.

3. Machine around the patch with two rows of zig-zag stitches.

4. Cut back the damaged cloth to the inside of the patch, and seal the cut edge with a hot knife.

Repairing spinnakers

The spinnaker is the sail which invariably receives most wear and tear. It used to be possible to repair the majority of spinnaker rips with self-adhesive spinnaker repair tape, but with the increasing use of highly resinated cloths it is a lot harder and tears have to be repaired by window patching.

When sewing a patch on a silicon-coated spinnaker, it may be necessary to hold the patch in place with dressmaking pins, if the double-sided tape is not sticking.

If the rip cuts right across one of the luff tapes, you will need to 're-fair' the luff. First patch the tear as before then pin the luff out flat to remove any wrinkles. It should now be possible to see the curved shape of the luff. Use a long sail batten to help re-draw the luff curve across the patched area. You may need to allow extra luff hollow to obtain a smooth and fair curve down the length of the luff.

WINTER OVERHAUL

You should be checking the condition of your sails all the time, but at the end of the season the sails of yachts, in particular, should be given a major overhaul. Rinse them off thoroughly and return them to the sailmaker, where they will be checked for areas of chafe, worn batten pockets, broken stitches and more major damage.

This is the time to have any sails rejuvenated. A stretched leech on a cross-cut Dacron mainsail can be easily cured with a few leech take-ups. Tell the sailmaker exactly where and how much the leech vibrates, so he can assess the amount and position of the take-up required. Laminate mainsails can be harder to adjust but similar take-ups can be added to the joining seams to increase the sail's competitive lifespan.

Old spinnakers can often be effectively doctored by fitting new leech tapes and short take-ups in the shoulders to round up the luffs, making the sail easier to trim. Check big spinnakers to make sure they have not stretched out of class. (Incidentally, always make sure spinnakers are completely dry when being measured in at a regatta as they 'grow' significantly when wet. If a kite is found to be oversize, ten minutes in a tumble dryer can easily take several inches off the luff measurement.)

The end of the season is the best time to review the entire sail inventory and decide which sails are still competitive and which have seen better days. Old sails can be kept for delivery trips, crew training or cut down for furling headsails or even sold.

All sails should be stored completely dry; seal them in plastic bags if you have to store them in a damp environment over the winter. Spray all metal fittings and sailbag zips with silicon if you want them to work again next time.

If your boat does need new sails for the forthcoming season, always try to order them in the autumn. The sail loft will have more time to devote to both you and the sails, and you can beat the annual price rise. You will also stand a better chance of receiving them in good time for the first race of the new season. Here's hoping you win it!

11 Asymmetric spinnakers

What is an asymmetric spinnaker?

The term 'asymmetric spinnaker' covers a surprisingly wide range of sail types. The common factor is their lack of symmetry about the centreline and the fact that they are reaching sails. Most asymmetrics (or 'gennakers' as some sail lofts like to brand them) have a leech length shorter than the luff and a mid-girth dimension the same or shorter than the foot length, which gives the sail its characteristic triangular look. However, it is also possible to design a sail which is symmetrical on the loft floor, but once flying takes up a draft-forward, asymmetric shape.

The modern asymmetric spinnaker was developed in the late 1980s, although the sails had been around a long time as cruising chutes on yachts and as racing kites on the Australian 18' Skiffs. The cruising chute was designed as a downwind sail for shorthanded sailing, with no need for a pole and being easy to gybe. Skiffs needed asymmetrics as soon as the boats became light enough to sail faster than the wind. As we saw in Chapter 1, a conventional spinnaker used downwind has almost no attached flow. Although the boat can head almost dead downwind, it can only do so at less than the true windspeed and forward thrust will only be a function of sail area and windspeed. To go faster you need to head up so the wind is on the beam, creating more attached flow which begins to improve the lift to drag ratio, increases boatspeed and builds the apparent windspeed. As the speed increases the apparent wind angle shifts forward, allowing the helmsman to bear off onto a more downwind angle, but still seemingly on a close reach with the apparent wind angle around 90-100 degrees. The stronger the breeze, the faster the boatspeed, the further forward the apparent wind swings and the lower the boat can sail. (In high winds, performance dinghies like skiffs and 49ers are forced to sail low just to balance the kite and keep the boat upright. You will often see them

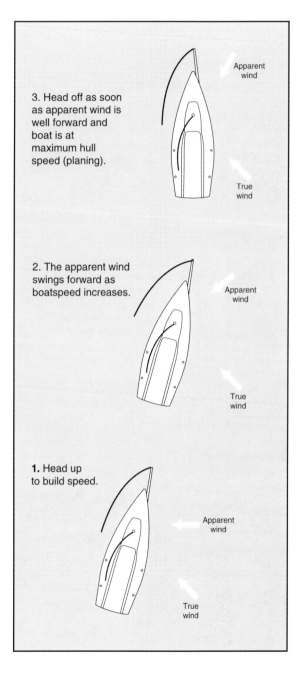

3. Head off as soon as apparent wind is well forward and boat is at maximum hull speed (planing).

Apparent wind

True wind

2. The apparent wind swings forward as boatspeed increases.

Apparent wind

True wind

1. Head up to build speed.

Apparent wind

True wind

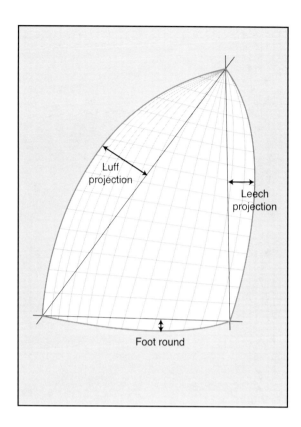

Luff projection

Leech projection

Foot round

pointing virtually dead downwind but with their sails set for a close reach because they are travelling so fast.)

SAIL SHAPE AND SIZE

There seems to be no common method of describing the relative dimensions of the asymmetric, so recent is its development. Most class rules control the size of the sail by limiting the mid-girth measurement to either a little more or a little less than the foot length and the luff length to 107% - 109% of the straight line distance from the end of the bowsprit to the top of the mast or halyard exit.

The basic shape of the sail is determined by the amount of luff projection, leech projection and foot round. A sail designed to run relatively deep downwind will have a maximum luff projection so that when the tack line is eased out the sail can roll round to windward, creating a greater projected sail area, away from the lee of the mainsail. To support this large luff projection the sail needs to be quite deep and draft-forward, otherwise the 'positive' area of the luff (all that

part of the sail beyond a straight line from tack to head) will simply fold inwards and flap. A close-reaching sail or one designed for heavy airs cannot afford to be so deep because it would cause too much drag and create large heeling forces. So a fast reaching asymmetric has less depth, can be less draft-forward and will necessarily carry less luff projection. The short-fall in girth measurement can be taken up by extending the leech so it is slightly 'positive' when laid flat on the floor. This can help to keep the back of the sail flat by levering open the leech, allowing the wind a free exit.

In the early days it was thought that two sizes of kite would be required in some classes: a full size, light to medium sail and also a flatter sail with a smaller girth and a higher clew for reaching in heavy airs. This was certainly the case in the Melges 24 class where two gennakers (large and small) were allowed to be carried aboard. As is the norm with new sail development, the good guys soon learnt that it paid to point the boat lower as the breeze increased and so could avoid becoming overpowered with the big kite up. As the Melges 24 class was mainly sailing windward/leeward courses, the development focus shifted to producing full-sized asymmetrics that would run deeper. Thus the second generation sails were created: 'knuckled fronted' deep sails with maximum luff projection, designed to be sailed with as much of the sail rolled to windward as possible. The class rules were then changed to permit carrying two large spinnakers.

As most one design classes have a maximum mid-girth rule, most of the asymmetric spinnaker development has been about finding the balance between depth, draft and the matching luff projection. Sails designed predominantly for heavy air reaching may also have a shorter luff length, around 105% of the straight line distance, rather than the more common 108-109 % of the all purpose/running asymmetric kite. This is because the sail will be sheeted harder and the luff comes under a greater load. The shorter luff length will help prevent the loaded sail sagging away to leeward. Some one design fleets are stuck with class rules which were drawn up when asymmetrics were in their infancy and limit what would now be considered the correct size and shape and can result in slightly odd-looking gennakers.

A displacement cruiser/racer asymmetric set

Tie rather than shackle the halyard block to allow it a fuller range of movement.

Strip the cover off the halyard to help it run, and attach a plastic ball to prevent the knot being pulled into the sheave.

on a bowsprit will generally be fuller, with a maximum luff projection so that the boat can sail as low as possible downwind when competing against symmetrical spinnakers in handicap racing. Some conventionally-rigged race boats without a bowsprit will carry an asymmetric sail as a specialised reaching sail for offshore races, set flying from the spinnaker pole fixed low on the mast. Such a sail can't be as big or as zeffective as a kite set from a bowsprit, but will be a more efficient reaching sail than a conventional spinnaker. Rating-wise the smaller kite will be more in keeping with the measurements of the rest of the spinnaker inventory and will not usually attract any extra rating penalty.

Choosing the right sail for your boat

The degree of decision making when ordering your new asymmetric will vary dramatically with the type of boat. In strictly controlled one design dinghy classes such as the 49er, Laser 4000 and Laser 5000 you will be lucky to have even a choice of colour, whereas the Melges 24 class has a greater range of options. But most sailors opt for either a full size running sail or a slightly flatter reaching kite with less luff projection, depending on the type of course to be sailed. The Ultra 30 class has no rules at all on spinnaker size. It used to be said in the fleet that big was not always best, but over the years the sails and handling techniques have developed to the stage where all the gennakers in the fleet are a similar size, with girths of around 75-80% of the luff length (limited only by the sheeting position on the boat) and with a relatively high

clew as only one sail is allowed and it therefore has to be all-purpose.

The most important factor to consider is the type of racing you want to use the sail for. If are sailing a sportsboat on predominantly windward/leeward courses you need a full, knuckle fronted sail with the biggest possible luff projection to help you sail as low as possible when the conditions are right. It is hard to give advice on the best choice of sail for the handicap classes, as rules such as IRC, PHRF, IMS and the new IRM all seem to change regularly. The current IMS rule does not favour sprit boats as it considers the bowsprit to be angled aft just like a conventional pole and so overestimates the boatspeed in displacement mode and underestimates it in planning conditions.

Whatever the rating rule, work out any extra penalty from adding an asymmetric to the downwind inventory and then see if the boat can sail to the increased rating. Consider also how long your extra sail is likely to be used on the racecourse.

RIGGING TIPS FOR SMOOTHER HANDLING

As the gennaker is flown out of reach at the end of the bowsprit, it is worth spending a few moments at the dock ensuring it is rigged properly, ie check the retrieval line is correctly-routed and the sail packed without a twist. On a high performance dinghy, if the sail goes up and a line is rigged wrongly there is often little chance of avoiding an early bath, so develop a mental check list for the correct order of rigging every time you go afloat. One tip for smoother

Two marks on the tack line show where to tie it to the sail for medium and light conditions. By tying to the second mark the sail flies higher in light airs.

gybing is that the halyard block at the top of the mast must be able to swivel freely to allow the head of the kite to twist through in the gybe and be free to spin out any twists during the hoist. In the photo the block has been tied onto the eye on the mast rather than using a shackle for this very reason. Ideally the block wants to be held as high up but as far out from the mast as allowed by class rules to hold the sail as far away from the rig as possible to facilitate gybing.

When you're rigging the sail attach the halyard first and mark it to show the fully-up position. Put the mark where you can see it when hoisting frantically: ideally at the cleat/clutch or where it exits the mast. On skiff-type dinghies with heavily pre-bent rigs the halyard is really tough to raise due to the friction against the inside wall of the contorted spar. Some 49er sailors sought to solve the problem by rigging an external halyard but this was ruled illegal and so the top guys now strip the cover off the Spectra/Dyneema halyard to expose the soft, slinky core which is thinner and runs more easily and also reduces the weight aloft. The polyester cover is left on where the halyard exits the mast to ease handling and to grip in the cleat. On all asymmetric boats it is well worth fitting a colour-coded plastic ball to the end of the halyard. This prevents the knot being pulled into the sheave and a consistent halyard setting is achieved on every hoist. On a cruiser/racer there are likely to be two kite halyards and two genoa halyards, all with their covers removed to run faster and save weight and all looking identical when clipped down at the base of the mast. To make life easier for the bow and mast persons it is a good idea to

match the colour of the plastic ball on the end of the halyard with the colour of the tail back in the cockpit. That way, the bowman faced with a sail change or hoist in rough conditions will know exactly which halyard both he and the mastman are talking about.

Having tied on the halyard, next chase down the luff to check for twists and then tie the tack line on with a bowline to a pre-determined mark so that it is either tight to the end of the pole for medium and breezy conditions or set flying a few inches off the pole for running deep in light airs. Sportsboats like the Melges have the tack line adjustable in the cockpit so always tie it onto the tack in the same position so that marks at the cleat end are reproducible.

Next attach the retrieval or downhaul line (often the other end of the halyard), ideally with a lightweight tapered end. On the 49er it runs from the leeward side of the spinnaker, through the bottom patch, up the inside and out again. Just before the second patch tie a stopper knot and fit a plastic ball on the 'outside' of the spinnaker. The knot acts as a spacer on the retrieval line and prevents the kite forming a big heavy lump of nylon when hauled into the sock. The length of the spacer should be set so that when the stopper knot comes up against the inner end of the spinnaker sock, the clews of the sail are just disappearing into the mouth of the chute. At this stage attach the gennaker sheets. You may be able to use a small shackle to make changing kites easier (a practice outlawed on the 49er but still used on other boats such as the Laser 5000), and a short length of rope sewn and taped over to create a smooth

Rigging the asymmetric retrieval line. This concertinas the sail neatly so it will fit into the sock. Note the bobble to prevent bunching.

Sew a length of thin line onto the sheet to prevent the shackle (or knot) catching on the forestay, and shackle the sail to this line. Tape the join.

Tie the two ends of the sheet together. It's then easy to grab the sheet in a gybe. The knots act as a stopper against the spinnaker turning block so you can use the sheet as a righting line after the inevitable capsize!

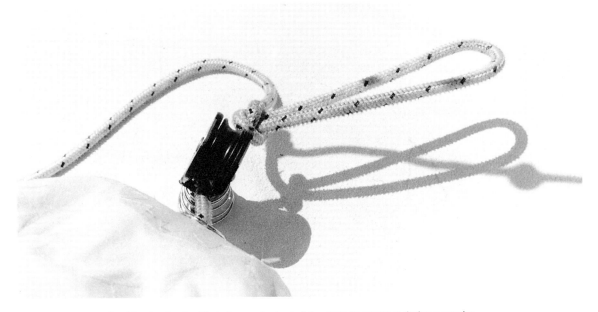

Put a hitch in the retrieval line to stop the kite being washed out of the chute in waves or during a capsize.

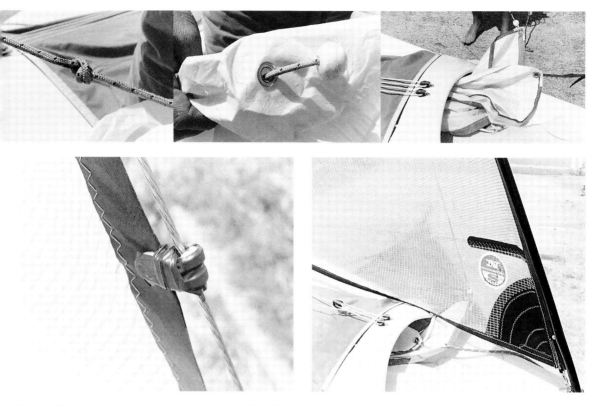

**Tape up the lower jib hanks to prevent the sheet catching. Fit a plastic tube around the bottom of the forestay.
On a drop, this will help the asymmetric around the forestay and into the chute.**

bridge across the knot or loop to prevent the sheets from catching on the forestay during a gybe. You can try the same trick on sportsboats but if not make sure you use the smallest knot to minimise the chances of its catching and stopping you gybing. Tying the ends of the kite sheets together makes it easier to grab hold of the tail and has the added advantage of acting as a stopper knot against the spinnaker block for use as a righting line in the event of a capsize ......often an inevitable occurrence in 49er racing! Arrange the sheets in the boat so that they won't get washed over the gunwale and trail overboard or out of the back of the boat. Some sportsboats use a velcro loop to secure and tidy the sheets next to the final turning block so that the sheet is always to hand and will come free easily as the sail is hoisted.

Another rigging tip for heavy air survival conditions is to put a loose hitch in the spinnaker retrieval line just aft of the block, to stop the kite floating out of the chute after a capsize or being dragged out by waves. A quick pull on the end of the rope will release the line prior to the hoist. Finally tape up any sharp fittings at the head and tack of the jib to avoid expensive rips in the kite, (especially the lower two or three jib hanks) and consider fitting a length of split plastic tube over the forestay to make it easier to drag the sail in on the gybe where the retrieval line has to go round to windward of the forestay.

It is well worth hoisting the sail in the dinghy park just to check that all the lines are led correctly and that the halyard is not twisted around the forestay. Then drop it carefully and twist-free into the chute, ready for a perfect first hoist. On a sportsboat or keelboat launch the kite on the way out to the start; the leeward mark is not the place to find out that the downhaul has been looped around the forestay and the kite won't come down!

A leeward hoist from a chute. See text for details.

TECHNIQUE

Hoisting the kite

The techniques for hoisting, dropping and gybing an asymmetric spinnaker all vary between different types of boat, and within one design fleets from crew to crew. The two examples I have used here come from the 49er Olympic dinghy and the Melges 24 sportsboat, and the techniques described may have to be altered slightly to accommodate the different class rules and layouts of other boats.

Hoisting the kite on the 49er and similar skiff-type boats is relatively straightforward provided the boat has borne away and is balanced before the crew goes for the hoist. Upwind it is usual for the 49er crew to take the mainsheet, so the first move prior to the hoist is to pass the mainsheet back to the helm. As the crew comes in from the trapeze and moves into the boat he/she eases the vang and the jibsheets to settings for the reach. It is critical for the helmsman to take over the balance of the boat at this point and, depending on the wind strength, will either have to move forward to keep the bow in and the boat planing or aft if there is a danger of the nose burying. To keep the boat flat and the foils in the water luff to make the boat heel or bear off to make it roll to weather. As in all breezy downwind sailing the trick is to keep the rig under the boat.

The crew then hoists the gennaker as quickly as possible to avoid any danger of the of the sail falling in the water and keeps hauling away until the mark on the halyard reaches the cleat. This is important as without a mark it is hard to know when the sail is fully hoisted. Once the asymmetric has filled the halyard load can be enormous and it will be hard to raise the remaining half metre or so without first collapsing the kite. Once the sail is hoisted the crew grabs the sheet, moves onto the wing, hooks on and jumps out onto the wire.

When it comes to hoisting the gennaker on a sportsboat or cruiser/racer, the main concern is avoiding the sail falling in the water. If this happens the crew at the back of the boat has about two seconds in which to pluck up the wet mass of nylon as it slides past to leeward, before it becomes a huge sea anchor which then invariably rips! This can happen easily, especially on a sportsboat where hoisting from the rail means the sail is dangerously close to the water and there is often not the luxury of a spare pair of hands to hold the spinnaker as it goes up. The way to avoid a trawl is to hoist as fast as possible while at the same time pulling the tack out to the end of the bowsprit, away from the lee of the headsail so the kite can fill quickly and lift clear of the water. The photo sequence on pages 104-5 shows how important it is to get the sail filled quickly so that it does not twist, wrap or get sucked into the back of the mainsail and become jammed inside the shrouds. The Melges 24 has a much shorter bowsprit than the 49er which makes it harder to get the sail out from behind the jib. Note how, in the sequence, the helmsman luffs to help fill the chute, but then it suddenly fills with a bang, so he has to be ready to dump the main and head off to keep the boat upright, before building speed and settling onto the optimum VMG course. The Melges

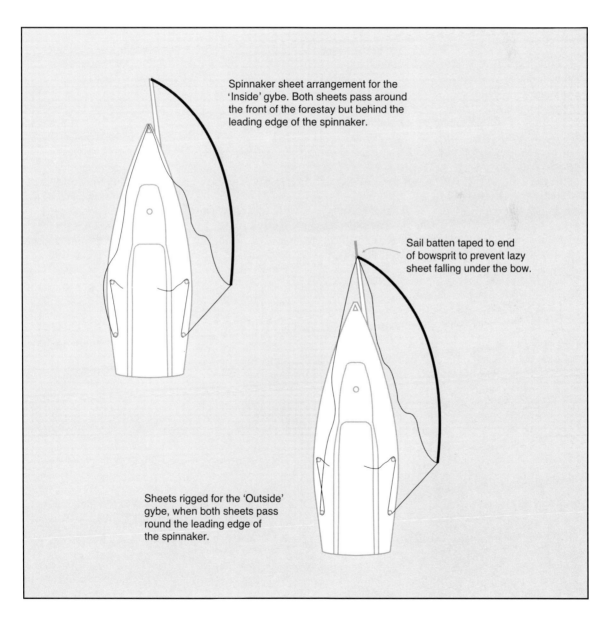

Spinnaker sheet arrangement for the 'Inside' gybe. Both sheets pass around the front of the forestay but behind the leading edge of the spinnaker.

Sail batten taped to end of bowsprit to prevent lazy sheet falling under the bow.

Sheets rigged for the 'Outside' gybe, when both sheets pass round the leading edge of the spinnaker.

Hoisting on a sportsboat. Bear away, hoist fast and luff to fill the kite (but be ready for a big bear away as it fills, to keep the boat flat).

crews have the choice of hoisting the kite through the shrouds, (which is faster), or round the back of the shrouds, which is slower but reduces the risk of the head of the sail jamming between the shrouds and the mast. You will need to work out the exact sequence of events that suits your boat best.

To speed up the hoist on a keelboat with a retracting bowsprit, pre-set the tack line before the hoist so that the foot of the sail is automatically dragged forward as the pole is launched and the tack arrives at the end of the pole as soon as the sail is up, helping to fill the sail quickly and also preventing the base of the sail falling in the water. Similarly, the sheet can be pre-set in the cleat with two meters of slack

so that one crew member can hoist the halyard then turn around and pick up the sheet, trimming in the small amount of slack as he moves out to the rail.

Gybing a keelboat

One of the main benefits of racing with an asymmetric spinnaker is the ease of gybing. Simply let one sheet go and pull in the other! However, on keelboats, where there is a great deal of free-flying nylon to move from one side of the boat to the other, there is a great opportunity for the for the sail to wrap.

There are in fact two methods of gybing the gennaker on a keelboat: inside, when the spinnaker sheets pass around the front of the

Gybing a sportsboat. Overtrim into the gybe to avoid a wrap, then pull hard on the new sheet.

forestay but behind the leading edge of the spinnaker, and outside, when the sheets are rigged to run outside of both ie round in front of the spinnaker luff. The "outside" method was used primarily in the early days of learning how to handle the asymmetric kite and was considered the safer option because the sail was released and billowed around the front of the boat before being pulled in on the new side with little chance of it causing a wrap or the boat being knocked down if caught by a gust. It was very much a stop-and-start-again gybe and is still used by many crews in heavy airs when the chance of the sail catching and pinning the boat

during an inside gybe is too great to risk. It's also good on boats with a short bowsprit where it is tough to get a large area of spinnaker cloth to pass through between the forestay and spinnaker luff. For novice crews unused to handling a large asymmetric it may be best to begin gybing 'outside', before moving on to the 'inside' method. The 'inside' gybe is a much quicker turn as there is a lot less sheet to pull through and the power is kept on throughout. Co-ordination of the turn and the rapid sheeting in of the sail on the new gybe are the keys to avoiding twisting or wrapping the sail around the forestay. The gybing photo sequence shows

Gybing a 49er. See text for details.

how once the gybe is called, the boat bears off
and the kite trimmer moves into the middle of
the boat in preparation. He/she keeps hold of the
old sheet, slightly over-trimmed to keep the sail
pulling and to help avoid a wrap, and then starts
hauling hard on the new sheet to pull the clew
of the sail across the boat. The trick here for
the helmsman is to follow the movement of the
spinnaker with the tiller and wait for the clew
of the kite to cross the forestay before the stern
passes through the eye of the wind. This way the
sail remains powered up and creates sufficient
load in the sail to help "pop" the head the right
way round. In light airs getting the head to rotate

cleanly without wrapping is difficult and can be
aided by:
● sailing higher angles into and out
of the gybe
● the foredeck crew giving a sharp tug
down the leech of the gennaker as it crosses
the boat
● the foredeck crew then helping to pull
through the slack on the old kite sheet
so that the clew is not slowed as it crosses
the boat.

Depending on the wind strength, the helmsman
should come out of the gybe slightly high to

Dropping to windward.

build flow across the sail to help it fill before heading back to the optimum VMG course.

What to do if you get a wrap

If a wrap does occur and looks unlikely to come out with a few sharp pulls, the quickest way out is to gybe back onto the old course as soon as you realise the problem, build speed and then try again. Holding onto a twisted sail will only make the wrap tighter and may cause damage to the sail. If the proximity of other boats prevents your gybing back the only option is to blow several meters of spinnaker halyard, which lets the kite fly away from the boat. The crew should now be able to free the twist by pulling down

on the leech. The crew at the front of the boat can help by keeping an eye on the head of the sail and calling when it has 'popped through' cleanly, as the trimmer may have his work cut out hauling in the new sheet and will be focusing on the clew of the sail. If all else fails, lower the sail onto the foredeck until the crew can reach the problem and unwrap the twist by hand.

Gybing a dinghy

Dinghies like the 49er need the boat to be well balanced before you gybe. Ideally go for it when the boat is on the plane to reduce the loads on the rig, making it easier to pull the sails across. In really light conditions it will pay to roll the boat

A Kiwi drop.

to windward, just like a roll tack, to help the sails through the gybe. The 49er gybing photo sequence (pages 106-7) shows how the crew comes in from the wire fractionally before the helm to organise the sheets and uncleat the jib (if necessary – on the 49er the jib is self tacking). The helm bears away to balance the crew's weight and on the call the crew releases the old sheet and hauls like crazy on the new one. The art of avoiding a twist is not to let out the old sheet prematurely so that it blows forward and wraps itself. Hold it over-trimmed a little into the gybe, so the clew has the shortest distance to travel as soon as the helm throws the boom over, and then sheet in as fast as possible to get it filling on the new side. Aim to get the clew just kissing the forestay through the gybe, but the exact timing will alter with windspeed.

Be prepared to ease sheet rapidly as the gennaker fills suddenly or the boat will heel and the helm will need to bear off to balance the boat. The crew must jump out on the wire and sheet in as soon as possible. Once balanced and in control the helmsman luffs up to the fast angle – and away you go!

The drop

Coming in to the bottom mark, a keelboat crew needs to plan ahead and work out which side the next hoist is likely to be, so that the drop can be made on that side. (In a weight-conscious boat there is no time to have someone down to leeward changing over the spinnaker gear.) The simplest option is a leeward takedown where the order of events is first to let the bowsprit in and/or the tackline, releasing the tack of the sail so it can collapse in the lee of the mainsail. From here the bowman can catch hold of the foot and gather in several armfuls towards the tack, before the halyard is released and the sail pulled down and stuffed into the bag. On larger cruiser/racers it may be easier to fit a tack retrieval line to haul the tack of the sail back into the boat quickly.

Dropping a large keelboat kite to windward in

Dropping into a chute. See text for details.

any sort of a breeze can be tricky as the large area of sailcloth can get blown hard against the rig and headsail before you have time to get it in the bag. If you need to drop to windward it's better to plan your run in to the mark to allow for a last gybe at the buoy. This 'Kiwi Drop', as some call it, involves gybing the boat and dropping the gennaker at the same time, so that it comes down on what becomes the windward side. The technique needs to be well practised but basically the crew releases the bowsprit (and tackline if it is separate) as the helm turns the boat, and the foredeck crew sitting to leeward collects the foot of the sail before the halyard is quickly blown. The forward crew is then free to sort and pack the sail from his sitting out position which has now become the windward side after the gybe, while the rest of the team sheet in and harden up around the mark.

Dropping the kite on a high performance trapeze dinghy is a whole lot simpler if the boat has a chute, like the 49er and International 14. The crew first hands the helmsman the spinnaker sheet before he moves into the middle of the boat, so that the kite is kept flying a few moments longer. The helm has to balance the shift in weight and bears off while the crew picks up the tail of the retrieval line, checks the halyard is free to run, opens the cleat to drop the halyard and then pulls as fast as he can on the retrieval line. Make sure your systems do not allow the sheets, halyard or pole inhaul to re-cleat themselves as the line runs through. Once the gennaker is safely tucked inside the chute, the crew trims the jib to the upwind setting, moves out onto the wing, clips on and takes back the mainsheet from the helmsman as he slides out on the wire. For asymmetric dinghies with bags, such as the 18 Foot Skiff and Laser 5000, the drop is usually done to windward to avoid having the crew down to leeward, except in the lightest of breezes when weight is not so critical. Try the keelboat technique of firing off the pole and collecting the foot of the sail first, before blowing the halyard, because this helps to collapse the sail and makes it easier and quicker to force into the bag.

Trimming the asymmetric

Trimming the gennaker on a dinghy is very straightforward compared to the mysterious art of conventional spinnaker trim: just let it out until the luff curls, then trim in! With no pole angle, pole height or tweaker controls to play with the key to going fast with the asymmetric lies more with the helmsman and his ability to pick the best wind angle and path through the waves. The sportsboat or keelboat trimmer has one more control at his command which widens the choice of angles to sail. In a medium breeze ease up the tack line and roll the boat to windward, Laser style, which helps the asymmetric fly further round to windward, creating a greater projected area and allowing the boat to head almost dead downwind. This is a handy technique on windward/leeward courses and when match racing. While trying to sail low like this, the trimmer's main objective is to ease the sheet as far as he can to float the sail out to windward as much as possible before the luff starts to roll inward. With the sail in this finely-balanced position it is then down to the helmsman to steer the boat to the spinnaker to keep it right on the edge.

As the breeze gets up it is vital to hike hard and move weight aft to keep the boat flat and planing fast. In heavy conditions be ready to dump the mainsail instantly by releasing both the vang and the mainsheet so that the whole sail inverts and flogs. Melges 24 sailors have an extra long tail on the vang control so that it can be played by a crew member standing behind the helmsman in extreme conditions. Ease the kite sheet as much as you dare without the sail collapsing . The helmsman can help the trimmer because he will feel when the rudder begins to load up and should then shout to the crew to ease sheets well before the foils stall out. This enables him to bear off to balance the helm.

TACTICS WITH THE ASYMMETRIC SPINNAKER

As this is primarily a book on sails and not race tactics, we will just have a brief look at the different style of tactics you need to think about when you start to race with an asymmetric spinnaker. Every boat has a set of angles and wind speeds at which its downwind VMG (see pages 82-83) will be much enhanced and in sprit boats this angle can be very specific, with a pronounced increase in performance. The key to getting down to the bottom mark before the other guys is to know the fastest angle for the current wind speed and then to adapt your strategy to spend as much of the leg as possible on that 'fast' angle.

The lighter and faster the boat the greater the differential in speed between the optimum VMG and sailing slightly off angle. The top Melges 24 sailors have now figured out that on the windward/leeward course in light airs the trick is to sail deep, running as low as possible with the tack line eased up and a big, 'knuckle fronted' kite projecting far to windward, helped by the boat being heeled in that direction too. Remember that gusts travel directly downwind, so the lower you go the longer you will stay with the pressure. In these conditions you have to overcome the urge to head up to make the boat feel 'pressured up', as the speed will increase but the VMG to the bottom mark may not. Rivals can always look good by heading up and reaching over the top of you, but a light airs downwind leg is like a game of chess with the winner only emerging at the bottom mark. In one design fleets such as the J 80, Melges 24, or 49er, the key is to monitor the rest of the fleet to find the angle that pays the best. Watch out for boats getting inside you and sliding past on a deeper track.

Once the breeze and waves build enough for the boat to plane, the game changes. Now it becomes a matter of hunting for the gusts that will keep you on the plane and maximise your downwind VMG. In order to 'stay with the pressure' the helmsman must be willing to listen to the trimmer calling the pressure that he feels through the sheet and to the tactician who should always be watching to weather for the next gust. The trimmer will make calls like "Pressure feels a bit soft here, come up a little," or, "Good pressure now, lets soak down a bit". Don't worry if this technique involves sailing an 'S' shaped course: the increase in VMG for a lightweight sportsboat should more than offset the extra distance sailed, but for a heavier displacement cruiser/racer the differential may not be so great and it will take a stronger breeze to make her get up and go.

The key technique here with all sprit boats (but most dramatically with the lightweight planing machines such as the 49er) is to sail high initially to build both the apparent wind speed and angle, before bearing off. On my first downwind ride on a 49er I had to be told when we were pointing almost straight downwind as with the huge asymmetric's sheet pulling hard and the main boom only just over the quarter it felt as though we were on a shy reach because our generated apparent wind was so far forward. The principle is the same for all asymmetric boats. As soon as there is enough wind for the boat to 'create its own wind', head up to build the apparent before coming off on a wave or with a gust. If the boat is capable of planing, the jump in VMG can be dramatic, as shown in the 'ear-lobe' shaped polar diagram of a Whitbread 60.

When looking to gybe and lay the mark, a useful rule of thumb is to wait until the mark is level with the helmsman or until he/she can see it over their shoulder. If in doubt allow a couple of extra boatlengths; understanding the mark is very slow as the opposition can reach in over the top of you and take your breeze. A gennaker produces a huge wind-shadow which can be used to great effect to get past another boat if you can reach up over the top of them. In this situation a kite that is flatter than your rival's will give you the advantage if a luffing match develops. Don't forget to pump the mainsail on each wave to promote surfing and give you the edge needed to sail over the other boat.

Racing with the asymmetric kite expands the sport of sailing and demands a whole new range of skills and experience. Downwind legs are no longer boring processions but exciting opportunities for great tactical battles. Enjoy!

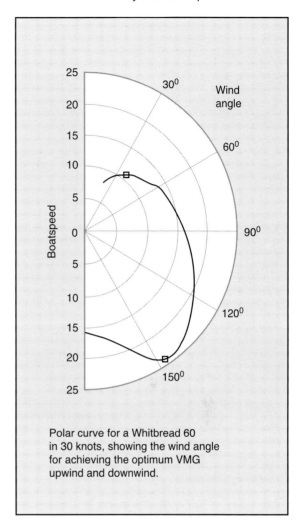

Polar curve for a Whitbread 60 in 30 knots, showing the wind angle for achieving the optimum VMG upwind and downwind.

Only the fast
know the feeling

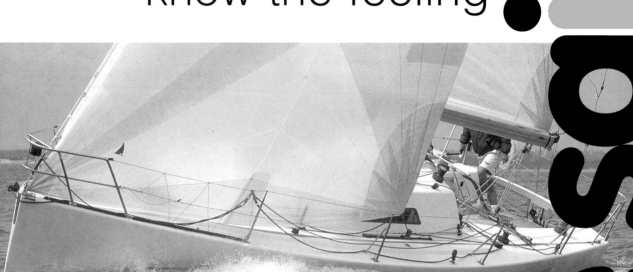

Photo: Rick Tomlinson.

You wind her up towards the line, the sails trim on perfectly,
the tactician's yelling the time in your ear - three, two, one - bang!
The bowman gives a thumbs up as he runs back down the deck.

'Sail your numbers,' whispers the tactician in your ear, 'there's a guy close to
leeward.' You take a quick glance, he's right there, jammed under your bow.
You were a touch late on the line, it's going to be tough. 'Big hike guys!' yells the
tactician. You settle her down, focus on nothing but the speed. A minute passes.
'It'll be OK,' you hear next. 'You're a little higher, little faster.' You risk another quick
glance. Bow to bow now, resigned looks from their crew. Then you hear, 'You got him,
he's toast.' 'Nice job back there.' says someone further up the rail.
You fight to hide the smile. Boatspeed. There's no other rush like it.

But you know the feeling, right? No? Then you're with the wrong sailmaker.
Get with the programme. Call Hyde today.

hyde sails

19 Hamble Yacht Services, Port Hamble
Hamble, Hants, SO31 4NN, England
Tel: 01703 454888. Fax: 01703 452753.
E-mail: TheSalesTeam@HydeSails.co.uk.
Web: http://hydesails.com.